America's Vice-Presidents

DIANA DIXON HEALY

America's Vice-Presidents

Our First Forty-three Vice-Presidents and How They Got to Be Number Two

ATHENEUM

New York

1984

Library of Congress Cataloging in Publication Data
Healy, Diana Dixon.
America's vice-presidents.
1. Vice-Presidents—United States—Biography.
2. United States—Politics and government. I. Title.
E176.49.H4 1984 973'.09'92 [B] 83-45490
ISBN 0-689-11454-0

Published simultaneously in Canada by McClelland and Stewart Ltd.
Manufactured by Fairfield Graphics, Fairfield, Pennsylvania
Composition by Maryland Linotype Composition Company,
Baltimore, Maryland
Designed by Mary Cregan
First Edition

DIANA DIXON HEALY

America's Vice-Presidents

Our First Forty-three Vice-Presidents and How They Got to Be Number Two

ATHENEUM

New York

1984

Library of Congress Cataloging in Publication Data
Healy, Diana Dixon.
America's vice-presidents.
1. Vice-Presidents—United States—Biography.
2. United States—Politics and government. I. Title.
E176.49.H4 1984 973'.09'92 [B] 83-45490
ISBN 0-689-11454-0

Published simultaneously in Canada by McClelland and Stewart Ltd.
Manufactured by Fairfield Graphics, Fairfield, Pennsylvania
Composition by Maryland Linotype Composition Company,
Baltimore, Maryland
Designed by Mary Cregan
First Edition

For Charlie

Contents

Contents

Contents

Preface

Woodrow Wilson wrote of the vice-presidency that "the chief embarrassment in describing it is that in saying how little there is to be said about it one has evidently said all that there is to say." This remains true of the office in spite of attempts to convince the electorate every four years that "this time it will be different." The office itself still officially consists of two time-wasting activities: presiding over the Senate and watching the president's health. Any role more challenging for the vice-president is completely at the discretion of the president, who often feels threatened by, alienated from, or too busy for his number-two man.

But some interesting characters have appeared in this vacuum: criminals, ambitious men, reluctant men, millionaires, men who were better qualified for the presidency than their leader, and those whose chances of succession caused a national shudder. There are only three ways in which all forty-three vice-presidents to date have been exactly the same. They have all been white, male, and (with the exception of Jefferson, a professed Deist) Christian.

There is a reason why it may be important to study the previous and present occupants of the vice-presidency and how they got there: thirteen of them have gone on to become, in one way or another, the president. The person we may disregard or scoff at in any given election year, because he or (in time, one presumes) she is relegated to the second spot on the ticket, has approximately one chance in three of eventually becoming our leader and the most powerful political figure in the world. *Caveat elector.*

Suggestions abound for improving the selection and status of the vice-president, including eliminating the office altogether. Supposing that it was agreed that a vice-president should be ideologically compatible, a geographical "balance," and capable of succeeding to the presidency, what then would be the best way to choose such a person and who should do the choosing? Should interested parties seek the nomination for the second office, campaigning for it as the presidential contenders do? If so, how would they present their qualifications to preside over the Senate without being laughed at? And wouldn't it be tactless to discuss how they would succeed if something (God forbid) should happen to the president? Maybe the person with the second greatest number of delegate votes at the nominating convention should automatically become the vice-presidential nominee—except that some unhappy combinations might occur because of the ideological differences within the same party (imagine a Humphrey–Thurmond ticket). There might also be a high incidence of outright refusals to take second place. An open convention such as the Democrats had in 1956, when Adlai E. Stevenson refused to choose his running mate, would make the selection somewhat more democratic, and Jimmy Carter's suggestion that the convention take thirty days to decide might help to eliminate some obvious lemons.

However the vice-presidency is filled, the office itself remains a puzzle. What can be done to make it more desirable, more responsible, and more of a training ground for a possible future president? As it now stands, we are in much the same situation as those who live in a monarchy—we must just hope for the best in our heir apparent.

Diana Dixon Healy
Wilton, Connecticut
October 1983

America's Vice-Presidents

John Adams

"His Royal Rotundity"

FEDERALIST
IN OFFICE: 1789–1797
PRESIDENT: GEORGE WASHINGTON

In the fledgling nation's first election, there was no differentiation between presidential and vice-presidential votes. All candidates were considered to be of presidential caliber. There were sixty-nine members of the first electoral college from the ten states that had so far ratified the Constitution. Each state was accorded as many electors as it had senators and representatives in Congress, but the method of choosing electors varied widely from state to state. Each state also had its own idea of who could do the choosing. Most states required of voters that they own land, slaves, money, or all of the above. "Those who own the country ought to govern it," said John Jay, expressing the sentiment of most of those in political life. Several states specifically withheld suffrage from atheists, Jews, or Roman Catholics.

Each elector could vote for two candidates. The man

JOHN ADAMS
(Artist: John Trumbull. National Portrait Gallery, Smithsonian Institution, Washington, D.C.)

emerging with the greatest number of votes would be president and, according to the Constitution, "after the choice of the President, the Person having the greatest number of Votes of the Electors shall be the Vice-President."

When John Adams saw that the election of 1788 would win him the vice-presidency with a total of 34 votes, instead of a unanimous 69, he complained to a friend: "Is not my election to this office in the scurvy manner in which it was done a curse rather than a blessing? Is this justice? Is there any common sense or decency in this business?"

Adams's dismay at being shortchanged 35 votes was such that he would have refused to take the office if he did not fear the "final failure of the government from my refusal." So he accepted but, like many a vice-president since that time, he was never happy in a position that he considered "not quite adapted to my character—I mean it is too inactive, and mechanical."

Adams had wanted to be our first president, and in different circumstances might have been so rewarded for his abilities and years of work in behalf of the Republic. But History had to be considered. It was important to elect a man who would look like the Father of His Country—a tall, dignified, and universally respected man, rather than a small, peppery, fat man, sometimes referred to as "His Royal Rotundity." Thus the unanimous choice for president was George Washington, not John Adams.

There were no official political parties at this time, but their future could be anticipated by a glance into the conflicting philosophies of the day. Alexander Hamilton spoke for Federalist views in advocating a strong central government that would not involve the "turbulent and changing" common people, who "seldom judge or determine right." Thomas Jefferson led the Anti-Federalists, or Republicans, who envisaged an agrarian nation with all men sharing in the job of government.

These sharply contrasting views helped produce a lively contest for the number-two spot in 1788. With Adams in the Federalist camp, the group led by Jefferson put forward New York governor George Clinton. Much of the support for Clinton (as well as for the other nine men who received second votes) came as the result of the work of that consummate backstage manipulator, Alexander Hamilton. Foreign-born, Hamilton could not run for president under the terms of the Constitution, but felt that if he could not be a king, he would be a kingmaker.

This "bastard brat of a Scotch pedlar" (according to Adams) sought to deflate Adams's influence by urging the electors to spread their second vote around, with the ostensible purpose of guaranteeing the election of Washington as president and avoiding the "possibility of rendering it doubtful who is appointed President." If Washington and Adams both received 69 votes, Congress would have to break the tie. Adams later wrote to a friend that "Hamilton had insinuated . . . that I should not harmonize with Washington, and (would you believe it?) that John Adams was a man of too much influence to be so near Washington. In this dark and insidious manner did this intriguer lay schemes in secret against me . . ."

Hamilton's "schemes" resulted in Adams's "scurvy" showing at the polls.

Actually, Washington had made it clear that he favored Adams for the vice-presidential spot in spite of Adams's past jealousies and what Hamilton called his "disgusting egotism" and "ungovernable indiscretion of . . . temper." There were others in this new democracy who expressed concern about Adams's love of titles. He assured critics that it was just a joke that he sometimes referred to himself as the "Duke of Braintree" (his Massachusetts home). But actually the man had little humor. He was known for his touchy vanity and curmudgeonly personality. And he was a cynic who believed that "men are never good but through necessity." Yet Adams's intelligence, honesty, and genuine patriotism insured that he had many supporters in addition to his devoted wife, Abigail. Jefferson considered him "as disinterested as the being who made him." Ben Franklin, in a mixed review, described him as "always an honest man, often a wise one, but sometimes, and in some things, wholly out of his senses."

The need for a vice-president had been called into question even as it was being written into the Constitution in 1787. Franklin asserted at the time that he was "against having a vice-president. If they insist upon having one, I shall address him as 'Your Superfluous Excellency.' "

Following the election, Adams's frustrations in trying to figure out just what his new job entailed were reflected in letters such as the one complaining, "My country has in its wisdom contrived for me the most insignificant office that ever the invention of man contrived or his imagination conceived." But he also realized the potential of the vice-presidency, saying, "I am vice-president. In this I am nothing, but I may be everything."

Present at the creation of a new government, Adams wanted to be certain that proper precedents were set for the future. One of his concerns was the question of how to address the president. If the simple title "President of the United States" was used, he feared that the common people of foreign countries would "despise him to all eternity." He was disappointed when the title proposed by a Senate committee, "His Highness, the President of the United States of America, and Protector of their Liberties," was rejected.

Adams also considered it his duty, while presiding over the Senate, to set the agenda, to express his own opinions during debates, and generally to act as leader of the Federalist majority. Since there were only twenty-two members of the original U.S. Senate, Adams had numerous opportunities to cast the tie-breaking vote. In fact, his record of 29 tie-breaking votes still stands for a vice-president. One important vote upheld the president's right to dismiss appointees without the approval of the Senate.

During his eight years in office, Adams increasingly felt forced to accept the role of passive observer that has become the norm for vice-presidents today. He once expressed his frustration in a letter, saying that he did not have "the smallest degree of power to do any good either in the executive, legislative, judicial departments. A mere Doge of Venice . . . a mere mechanical tool to wind up the clock."

Thomas Jefferson

The Leader of the Opposition

REPUBLICAN (ANTI-FEDERALIST)
IN OFFICE: 1797–1801
PRESIDENT: JOHN ADAMS

Thomas Jefferson should not have been vice-president; he was too good for the office. And, he was the leader of the emerging Republican, or Anti-Federalist, party—in opposition to that of President Adams. Nowadays a pairing of such dramatically opposed politicians on one ticket would be unthinkable. In reality, Jefferson and Adams felt a great deal of esteem and affection toward each other. It was their followers who turned the electioneering of 1796 into America's first all-out dirty campaign. The Federalists pictured Jefferson as an atheist, a coward, a drunkard, and a Jacobin who approved of the worst excesses of the French Revolution. The Anti-Federalists said Adams was a monarchist in love with titles and ceremonies, scheming to have one of his sons succeed him on the "throne."

After resigning as secretary of state during Washing-

THOMAS JEFFERSON
(Artist: François Jacques Dequevauviller. National Portrait Gallery, Smithsonian Institution, Washington, D.C.)

ton's administration, Jefferson had said, "Never again will I be enticed into politics." There is no doubt of his sincerity. He believed that "no man will ever bring out of that office [the presidency] the reputation which carries him into it. The honeymoon would be as short in that case as in any other, and its moments of ecstasy would be ransomed by years of torment and hatred."

Jefferson was also aware of the physical discomforts of high office in the eighteenth century. At that time, it meant getting to and from the capital by means of kidney-crushing rides in a stagecoach over primitive roads; months away from home and family; and before 1800, it meant living in Philadelphia—a city periodically decimated by yellow fever.

The election of 1796 was a particularly confusing one, due in large part to the Machiavellian Alexander Hamilton—that "evil genius of America" (according to Jefferson). The Federalists' candidates were Adams and Southerner Thomas Pinckney; the Republicans put up Jefferson and Aaron Burr. Hamilton publicly backed fellow Federalist Adams for the presidency while secretly pushing for Pinckney's election.

Hamilton felt that Pinckney had a "temper far more discreet and conciliatory than that of Mr. Adams," but what he may have meant was that Pinckney would be less independent and more open to "guidance." Adams's supporters countered Hamilton's machinations by casting their second votes for favorite-son candidates, thus assuring that Pinckney would not receive enough votes for the number-two spot. Adams received 71 votes and Pinckney 59, while the Anti-Federalists Jefferson and Burr got 68 and 30, making Jefferson vice-president.

Hamilton was sometimes too clever for his own good.

Jefferson had, of course, been intended for the presidency by his followers; James Madison, his strongest backer, avoided visiting him for a long time so as not to give him a chance to refuse the nomination. No one would accuse Jefferson of being naive though, but he did know that his name had been placed in opposition to that of his old Revolutionary compatriot, Adams. He claimed to believe that Adams deserved the presidency and hastened to assure him that he did "sincerely wish to be the second on that vote rather than the first . . . Ambition is long since dead in my mind. Yet even a well-weighed ambition would take the same side." Secretary of the Treasury Oliver Wolcott thought that this demonstrated "sufficient proof of some defect of character." But Jefferson was one of the few vice-presidents who claimed to feel that the "second office of this government [was] honorable and easy" and the first "but a splendid misery," and that it would give him an opportunity for "philosophical evenings in the winter and rural days in summer."

A true Republican, Jefferson wanted no formalities attached to his position and, before leaving for Philadelphia, he wrote to Madison that he would "escape into the city as covertly as possible. If Governor Mifflin [of Pennsylvania] should show any symptoms of ceremony, pray contrive to parry them." As an opposition leader, he probably realized the frustrations of not being consulted as to any government measures more than most would have, but he did not spend the next four years in mere philosophical contemplation.

Adams, either to be rid of him or because he was the

best man for the job (depending on the historian), asked Jefferson to undertake a mission to France. Jefferson refused on the ostensible grounds that it was not the province of vice-presidents to undertake foreign assignments, and it was a long time before a vice-president would go abroad. His real reasons for refusing, however, had more to do with the fact that he had no wish to aid Federalist policies. He also refused to attend cabinet meetings—a practice not changed until World War I.

While enduring the inactivity of the Senate's presiding officer, Jefferson had time to write the *Manual of Parliamentary Practice*, which, though unofficial, is still referred to in the Senate. He was also unwilling and unable to let his Republican sympathies lie dormant.

It was during the Adams administration that the Federalists dealt themselves a blow from which they would not recover: they passed the Alien Act and the Sedition Act. The Alien Act made it legal for the government to deport aliens they considered "dangerous"; that is, those who came in with strong Republican views. The Sedition Act made it a crime punishable by fine or imprisonment to "write, print, utter, or publish . . . any false, scandalous and malicious writing or writings against the government of the United States" or to speak of members of Congress or the President "with intent to defame [them] or to bring them . . . into contempt or disrepute." This made criminals of most articulate Republicans.

Jefferson, saying he didn't know which mortified him most—"that I should fear to write what I think, or my country bear such a state of things"—rose to the challenge in a way hard to imagine in latter-day vice-presidents. He secretly wrote the nine resolutions known as the Kentucky Resolves, which contended that the acts were unconstitutional and should be nullified. Kentucky and Virginia passed these resolves and declared the acts void in their states, striking an early blow for states' rights.

Jefferson's resolve to stay out of politics faded completely during his term as vice-president, and his letters to Madison show this turnaround. He began to lay plans to "cultivate Pennsylvania," whose votes would have made such a difference in the previous election, and logically wondered: "If one is to be a candidate, why not a successful one?"

Aaron Burr

A Biographer's Dream

REPUBLICAN
IN OFFICE: 1801–1805
PRESIDENT: THOMAS JEFFERSON

Aaron Burr was the only vice-president to commit murder while in office, at least the only one to our knowledge. It happened on the morning of July 11, 1804. Burr shot Alexander Hamilton on the heights of Weehawken, New Jersey, across the Hudson River from what is now 42nd Street in Manhattan.

The two men had been political enemies for thirty years, but Burr had taken special umbrage at a recently published report of Hamilton's insults, and so challenged him to the infamous duel. Dueling was not an unacceptable practice for settling arguments, but this time the winner decidedly became the loser. Burr, once much more popular than Hamilton, now was forced to flee public wrath, and Hamilton, whose son had also died in a duel, became a posthumous hero. Popular reaction to the tragedy was expressed in doggerel such as:

AARON BURR
(Artist: G. Parker. National Portrait Gallery, Smithsonian Institution, Washington, D.C.)

A Biographer's Dream

Oh Burr, oh Burr, what hast thou done,
Thou hast shooted dead great Hamilton!
You hid behind a bunch of thistle,
And shooted him dead with a great hoss pistol!

Even John Adams, who had good reason to dislike the man, said, "No one wished to get rid of Hamilton in that way." New Hampshire's senator William Plumer complained of the evil times when "the high office of President is filled by an infidel [referring to Jefferson], that of vice-president by a Murderer."

Handsome, brilliant, witty, a ladies' man, a man of action, inordinately ambitious, a rogue, and not always on good terms with the truth, Burr is a biographer's dream. He was the son of the minister who helped found Princeton University and grandson of the fire-breathing theologian Jonathan Edwards. But Burr strayed far from the pious beliefs of his forebears.

After honorable military service during the Revolution, Burr became prominent in New York politics as a Republican and the natural enemy of the Federalist power broker, Hamilton. When, in 1800, Jefferson and Burr again led the Republican ticket, it appeared certain they would beat the splintered Federalists led by John Adams and Charles Pinckney (Thomas's elder brother) in part because Adams was so unpopular as president and in part because of some dirty tricks by Hamilton that backfired. He had written a bitterly critical pamphlet about Adams and passed it out in secret to other Federalists, but Burr got hold of a copy and delighted in making it public.

So the two Republican candidates were winners. But there was a problem: they had won equally, each man receiving 73 votes. The tie threw the election into the Federalist-dominated House. Everyone knew that Jefferson had been slated for the top office and Burr for second, but there was room for mischief in the situation. Jefferson summed up the general feeling when he told Burr: "It was badly managed not to have arranged with certainty what seems to have been left to hazard."

Burr, who had the support of many Federalists because he was considered "a friend of the commercial interests" and was less likely to do away with marriage and to abolish churches than Jefferson—that "atheist in Religion and . . . fanatic in politics"—did not openly work for the presidency following the tie vote, but he did not concede either. In fact, he insisted that if the only way to break the tie was for him to assume the presidency, then, for the sake of the country, he would do it. Asked who would then be vice-president, he replied: "Jefferson." It is little wonder that Jefferson considered him a "crooked gun, or other perverted instrument, whose aim or shot you could never be sure of."

In Hamilton, however, Burr had a powerful opponent. In spite of his dislike of Jefferson, Hamilton acknowledged that he at least had "pretensions to character," while he viewed Burr as the "most unfit and dangerous man of the community." So he worked hard to make sure Burr did not become president, telling people, "If there be a man in the world I ought to hate, it is Jefferson. With Burr I have always been personally well. But the public good must be paramount to every private consideration."

It took 36 ballots and seven days of mounting tensions before the deadlock was finally broken in Jefferson's favor. At one point his backers even threatened to use armed force to see that right was done. Subsequent relations between president and vice-president were less than cordial. Burr's instincts told him he would rise no higher in his party and, indeed, he was passed over for a second term at the 1804 Republican caucus.

In April of that year, he sought and lost election as governor of New York on an independent ticket backed by disgruntled Federalists. Then, three months later, he met and killed his old foe on the cliffs of New Jersey. To avoid possible prosecution on a murder charge, he fled south and hid out for several months.

When the uproar about the duel had quieted down somewhat, Burr returned to Washington (where he was safe from extradition). He resumed his duties in the Senate and applied himself so diligently that he was considered by New York senator Samuel Mitchell to be "one of the best officers that ever presided over a deliberative assembly." On March 2, 1805, Burr delivered his farewell address to the Senate, speaking "with so much tenderness and concern that it wrought up the Senate in a most uncommon manner." He then "in a dignified manner walked to the door, which resounded as he with some force shut it after him . . . There was a solemn and silent weeping for perhaps five minutes."

Burr may have closed the door on his political career, but the man was not through yet. His next adventure involved a scheme to take over and rule a piece of the West, a project termed by Jefferson "the most extraordinary since the days of Don Quixote." Burr's true intentions are not clear, but they seemed treasonous, and he was arrested in 1806. Since there was no hard evidence and no real proof of a crime against the state, he was acquitted.

Burr spent the rest of his years in poverty, in and out of exile, but his life never grew boring. When, as an old man, he was questioned about the two illegitimate daughters under ten mentioned in his will, he replied, "When a lady sees fit to name me as the father of her children, why should I deny that honor?" And on the day he died, at eighty, his second wife's divorce from him became final—on the grounds of adultery.

George Clinton

An Early New York "Boss"

REPUBLICAN
IN OFFICE: 1805–1812
PRESIDENTS: THOMAS JEFFERSON,
JAMES MADISON

In the election fiasco of 1800, Aaron Burr almost stole the presidency from Jefferson. As a result of this, the Twelfth Amendment was passed in 1804. It required that separate ballots be held for president and vice-president. This eliminated the possibility of troublesome ties. At the same time it changed the character of the office of vice-president. With few exceptions, men nominated for the second post came now from the ranks of those who deserved a reward for party service or who filled a need for geographical or philosophical "balance" on the ticket.

The Twelfth Amendment did not please everyone. New Hampshire senator Plumer warned that "The Electors will not require those qualifications requisite for supreme command. The office [of vice-president] . . .

GEORGE CLINTON
(Collections of the Library of Congress)

will be a sinecure . . . exposed to sale to . . . aspiring candidates for the Presidency." And Connecticut congressman Roger Griswold prophesied that

> the man voted for as Vice-president will be selected without any decisive view to his qualifications to administer the government. The office will generally be carried into the market to be exchanged for the votes of some large state for President; and the only criterion which will be regarded as a qualification for the office of Vice-president will be the temporary influence of the candidate over the electors of his State.

This pessimistic attitude was proven right in 1804 with the election of George Clinton, and it was proven doubly right in 1808 with his reelection. If he had been elected ten or twenty years earlier, things might not have been so bad, but the man was sixty-five years old in 1804 and on the verge of senility.

One of this country's earliest "bosses," Clinton had controlled New York State politics from the time of the Revolution. He had served in the war as an undistinguished general but a rabid anti-Loyalist. One of his critics claimed that he had Loyalists "tarred and feathered, carted, shipped, fined, banished." Later Clinton sided with the Anti-Federalists in opposing a strong central government—not so much because he was a champion of the principles of states' rights but because it posed a threat to his personal fiefdom.

In 1795, after six terms as New York governor, Clinton retired because of ill health, tired mental faculties, and

—though loathe to admit it—declining popularity. In fact, in 1792, John Jay had beaten him in the election—until Clinton came up with a reason for invalidating the votes of three counties. In spite of his increasing decrepitude—or maybe because of it—Clinton wanted and thought he deserved the presidency. But when he realized in 1800 that he did not have a chance for either of the top offices against Jefferson and Burr, he ran for and won again the New York governorship.

After the passage of the Twelfth Amendment, Clinton had his chance in the election of 1804. The Republicans wanted a New Yorker to give geographical balance to a ticket led by Virginian Jefferson, and they may also have been looking for someone a little tamer than Aaron Burr to preside over the Senate. So, at age sixty-five, George Clinton got the nod for second place, which he hoped would be a stepping-stone to the presidency. The nearly extinct Federalist party had put up South Carolinian Charles Cotesworth Pinckney and Rufus King of New York.

The vice-presidency was not a happy experience for Clinton. Senator Plumer complained that Clinton was "old, feeble and altogether uncapable of the duty of presiding in the Senate" and that he had "no intellect—no memory." He would forget questions, miscount votes, or declare a vote before it was taken. John Quincy Adams wrote that Clinton was "totally ignorant of all the most common forms of proceeding in the Senate . . . a worse choice than Mr. Clinton could scarcely have been made." Virginia senator William Giles declared that if Clinton's cronies "had sent him here with a view to push him on to the Presidency, they had been unlucky in the choice of their expedient. It was a dangerous experiment . . . for in such conspicuous stations a man was apt to be seen through."

Clinton himself hated living in Washington and spent increasing amounts of time at home in New York. Of his job in the Senate, he complained that "sitting three hours in the chair at a time was extremely fatiguing" to him; and he wanted to be told when long speeches were coming so that he could go and "warm himself at the fire."

It seems reasonable to assume that with all this mutual displeasure, Clinton would have been quietly put out to pasture at the end of his first term—but no. At the next Republican caucus (1808), still coveting the highest office, George made his availability known but had no chance against Jefferson's choice for president, James Madison. The Republicans were, however, willing to nominate him for vice-president, so he made a bid as candidate for both offices—not too odd for a man who had once been both governor and lieutenant governor of New York at the same time.

When he lost the top spot on the ticket to Madison by a vote of 122 to 6, Clinton ranted about being "treated with great disrespect and cruelty by the gentlemen of his own party." He *did* win the nomination for the vice-presidency, with 113 votes, but was crankier than ever after the election, which the party won. He even refused to attend Madison's inauguration. Openly antagonistic to Madison and his policies, one of Clinton's final acts of pique was voting against renewing the United States Bank in 1811, legislation that Madison favored. This left the United States with no credit source to prepare for the War of 1812, the war against Britain which was fought for "Free Trade and Sailors' Rights" and from which came "The Star-Spangled Banner" and the first feelings of American invincibility.

None of this concerned Clinton, since he died in office (April 20, 1812), the first vice-president to do so.

Elbridge Gerry

"A Good War Will Help Us"

REPUBLICAN

IN OFFICE: 1813–1814

PRESIDENT: JAMES MADISON

In 1812, the Republicans looked to the North again for a running mate for Virginian James Madison. Since a Virginia–New York combination had worked before, their first stop was New York City. Here they broached the subject with George Clinton's nephew, DeWitt, another state "boss." When the younger Clinton refused the second spot, a caucus nominated John Langdon of New Hampshire. Langdon, who deserves a special place in vice-presidential history for having whatever it takes to turn down the nomination, claimed he was too old for it at seventy. So the caucus reconvened and gave the nod to a younger man, Elbridge Gerry, who was only sixty-eight.

Gerry's most noteworthy characteristic may have been his inconsistency. He was a rabid Republican who once said, "The whole business of life [is] what is best done

ELBRIDGE GERRY
(Artist: James Barton Longacre. National Portrait Gallery, Smithsonian Institution, Washington, D.C.)

for our country," but he basically disliked and distrusted the common man and felt that he should be denied the vote. Gerry was a signer of the Declaration of Independence, but he refused to sign the Constitution because of certain "details of the instrument." And he opposed the idea of a vice-president because "the close intimacy that must subsist between the President and Vice-President makes [such a duty] absolutely improper."

He was also vain, suspicious, and irritable. His good friend John Adams had to admit that he had "an obstinacy that will risk grave things to secure small ones" and that he "opposed everything he did not propose." Another contemporary, describing Gerry's speaking abilities, said he was "hesitating and laborious" and went "extensively into all subjects . . . without respect to elegance or flower of diction." A bit of a prude, Gerry urged that the "corrupt man and libertine" Ben Franklin be recalled from France and that stage plays be prohibited in Massachusetts.

Although he was a Harvard graduate, Gerry was unlike most vice-presidents in not having a law degree. He had chosen instead to go into business with his father and became wealthy as a shipper and sometime privateer. In 1797, President Adams appointed him to a three-man commission to settle some outstanding disputes with France, especially those concerning the seizure of American ships. Out of this came the XYZ affair.

When Gerry and the other commissioners, John Marshall and Charles Pinckney, arrived in France they were approached by representatives ("Messrs. X, Y, and Z") of the minister of foreign affairs, Talleyrand, who demanded $250,000 in cash and a $10,000 loan as payment for the end of the disputes and for the avoidance of war. An irate Pinckney told them, "No; no; not a sixpence!" and he and Marshall sailed for home, where their forthright stand against blackmail gave birth to one of America's favorite cries of defiance: "Millions for defense but not one cent for tribute!" Gerry decided to stay behind to see if he, being something of a Francophile, could work something out with Talleyrand on his own. Nothing was accomplished, although he later claimed that his continued presence in France prevented war. His critics took a dimmer view of his foreign dealings. Pinckney said that he had never "met a man of less candor and as much duplicity."

Massachusetts Republicans apparently accepted Gerry's version of himself as a peacemaker and nominated him for the one-year term of governor of the state four years in a row—1800–1803. But after going down to defeat in the general election four times, Gerry declared he was "tired of carrying the vain hope," and gave it up until 1810. Then he was victorious over the "most unpopular man in the state," Christopher Gore, and served two terms before being defeated again. At this point, he was nominated for vice-president. DeWitt Clinton, who had put together a coalition of dissatisfied Republicans and the remnants of the Federalists, and Pennsylvania Federalist Jared Ingersoll unsuccessfully opposed Madison and Gerry.

Gerry was a lackluster vice-president who dutifully presided in the Senate in spite of ill health. Some months after the inauguration, he came close to succeeding to the presidency. Madison was near death from fever for a time in 1813, the result of which would have been (according to one foreign minister in Washington) "a veritable national calamity. The President [Elbridge Gerry] who would succeed him for three and a half years is a respectable old man, but weak and worn out."

Gerry approved of the War of 1812, which raged during his term in office, saying, "We have been at peace too long, a good war will help us." The British pretty much ignored the old hawk in his rooms as they moved through Washington with their torches, burning the Capitol and the White House, and he died of a lung hemorrhage just one month before the Treaty of Ghent ended the hostilities in December 1814.

Another death which occurred at about the same time was that of Federalism. The Federalists of New England, who opposed the war, met at the Hartford Convention in 1814 to draw up a list of grievances to present to the government. Before their message could reach Washington, the treaty had been signed and a newly patriotic country saw their efforts as treasonous. The party never recovered.

Gerry's death left the vice-presidency vacant for the second time in three years; and this time the vacuum lasted for almost three years. The man's name, however, will always be part of our country's political vocabulary, thanks to an event that occurred during his second term as Massachusetts governor. Gerry and his Republican legislature came up with a redistricting plan that would insure a healthy majority of Republican voters over Federalists in one county. On the map, the outlines of this new district resembled a salamander. By combining salamander and the name of the governor who signed the plan into law, pundits created the term still used today for redistricting abuse: gerrymander.

Daniel D. Tompkins

Victim of "Pecuniary Embarrassments"

REPUBLICAN
IN OFFICE: 1817–1825
PRESIDENT: JAMES MONROE

The deaths of two successive elderly vice-presidents in office finally led the Republican leaders to put a little more thought into the selection of their next candidate. Their choice, forty-two-year-old Daniel Tompkins, was younger than his predecessors by two decades and seemed certain to have a long political life ahead of him. When he died just three months after leaving office, it began to look as if the office of vice-president itself had a curse hanging over it.

The son of a farmer, Tompkins rose rapidly in New York politics thanks in part to early support from De-Witt Clinton. He was elected governor in 1807 when he was just thirty-three and won reelection three times.

During the War of 1812, while most New Englanders refused to participate in either the fighting or the funding for the conflict, Governor Tompkins of New York

DANIEL D. TOMPKINS
(Artist: T. Woolworth. Collections of the Library of Congress)

was "heart and soul for the war." He roused his state to action. As dispersing agent for both New York State and the federal government, he raised millions of dollars, sometimes using merely his signature for collateral. President Madison thought highly enough of his efforts to offer Tompkins the job of secretary of state in late 1814. Tompkins felt he could do more for the war effort in New York, and refused.

On the domestic front, Tompkins was a liberal, working to abolish slavery in the state and to see that Indians were treated more humanely. A compleat politician, he "never forgot the name or face of anyone with whom he had converse," and he could charm women—still nonvoters but not without influence. Senator Jeremiah Mason claimed that "his capacity for friendship depended upon whether the success of his own career was endangered by the association."

Tompkins's ambitions were great. He wanted to be president in 1816, but Madison supported James Monroe as his successor, and that was that. Tompkins, not well enough known outside New York, did not receive a single vote for the nomination. He was offered the consolation prize, thus bringing another Virginia–New York alliance to Washington.

During Tompkins's two terms in office, some exciting and far-reaching changes took place in the country. The Erie Canal was completed. The West was attracting adventurous settlers who would one day cause new political alliances to be formed. Spain relinquished control of Florida. The Monroe Doctrine, warning that European colonization would no longer be tolerated in the Western Hemisphere, was issued. In the Congress and the cabinet,

Henry Clay, Daniel Webster, and John C. Calhoun were forming their reputations as powerful speakers. The Missouri Compromise (1820) postponed civil strife between North and South for many years. For a brief spell, we were essentially a one-party nation and the lack of political rancor gave the decade its name: Era of Good Feelings.

Unfortunately, the good feelings did not extend to Tompkins. After he became vice-president, news came out that he had apparently made a financial muddle of his fund-raising during the war. Some said that it was his erstwhile ally, DeWitt Clinton, who caused the spotlight to focus on Tompkins's imperfect bookkeeping skills—in retaliation for Tompkins's running against him for New York governor in 1820 and almost beating him. Whatever the case, Tompkins was $120,000 short in his accounting and was forced to spend most of his eight years in office trying to prove that he had not pocketed the money. The stress of attempting to clear his name led to some heavy drinking by Tompkins. He was termed a "degraded sot," and one observer said that "he was several times so drunk in the chair [of the Senate] that he could with difficulty put the questions."

Tompkins began to spend most of his time in his home state wrestling with his problems and was not even in Washington for his second inauguration. He was so rarely in the Senate that in 1823, a Senate president pro tempore had to be selected, and Tompkins never presided again. The next year, ill and worn-out, he assured Secretary of State John Quincy Adams that "he had no intention of being a candidate either for election to the presidency or for re-election as Vice-President. All he wanted was justice . . . had determined to take no part in the approaching election, and wished for nothing here after but quiet and retirement."

His wish came true. Tompkins died a year later of exhaustion, caused, as he said, by "toilsome days, sleepless nights, anxious cares, domestic bereavements, impaired constitution, debilitated body, unjust abuse and censure and accumulated pecuniary embarrassments."

Tompkins Square in New York City was later named for him in honor of the legislation abolishing slavery that Tompkins had signed during his governorship. His basic honesty was established when, upon further investigation of his fund-raising activities for the War of 1812, the government discovered that Tompkins was not in debt to it and was, in fact, owed several thousand dollars by the government. Many years later, this money was finally paid to his descendants.

John Caldwell Calhoun

Et tu, Brute?

REPUBLICAN
IN OFFICE: 1825–1832
PRESIDENTS: JOHN QUINCY ADAMS, ANDREW JACKSON

John C. Calhoun was our first vice-president to resign, beating Spiro Agnew to that dubious honor by 141 years. Calhoun's resignation was not the result of a criminal investigation, however, or accusations of immoral or unethical practices. Rather, it was because as vice-president he discovered that he had no forum for his views. The brilliant orator's need to speak was overwhelming, the words piling up behind his teeth. So nine weeks before the end of his second term, he resigned his seat at the front of the Senate and returned to the floor as senator.

A critic once said of Calhoun that he had "lax political principles and a disordinate ambition, [and was] not over delicate in the means of satisfying them." Certainly his ambition was high; he was aiming for the presidency and did not keep it a secret. Virginia senator John Randolph once showed his awareness of and contempt for

JOHN C. CALHOUN
(Artist: James Barton Longacre. National Portrait Gallery, Smithsonian Institution, Washington, D.C.)

this ambition by addressing Calhoun as "Mr. Vice-President, and would-be Mr. President of the United States, which God in his infinite mercy prevent."

In 1824, though only forty years old, Calhoun made his first bid for the nomination. But in a distinguished field that included John Quincy Adams and Andrew Jackson he was soon eliminated. Vice-president seemed to be the next best thing on his way to the top, and to make quite certain of winning that office Calhoun decided to run with both top contenders, Adams and Jackson, rather than risk choosing the wrong man. This in itself was ambitious, because now he would have to please Adams's friends in New England at the same time he was playing up to Jackson's rough Western crowd. He deserved to win.

Amid cries of "Foul!" Adams won a close election that had to be decided in the House, and Calhoun came with him for what was to be a very short honeymoon between the two men. Adams rebuffed Calhoun's various suggestions for cabinet appointments, and Calhoun retaliated by permitting and even encouraging attacks on the president from the Senate floor. When he was criticized for this passive act of ill will, he sanctimoniously replied, "I trust that it will never be the ambition of him who occupies this chair to enlarge its powers."

In Calhoun's day, the vice-president had the power to name senators to senatorial committees, but Calhoun ignored the choices of the administration. This seemed unfair even to one of Adams's strongest critics, Senator Randolph, and he saw to it that the vice-president was stripped of that prerogative. Adams and Calhoun then took to insulting each other in print, writing pseudonymous attacks in their favorite newspapers under the names "Patrick Henry" and "Onslow," respectively.

Adams's unpopularity extended beyond the vice-president's chair, and by 1828 it had become clear that Andrew Jackson would be the next president. Jackson's backers wooed Calhoun, thinking that his being anti-Adams meant being pro-Jackson, and convinced him to run for second spot again with tales of Jackson's nearly imminent demise and/or his determination to stay for just one term. This sounded pretty good to Calhoun, who was still a fairly young man and could wait a little longer.

But the Jackson supporters did not want Calhoun for vice-president simply because he looked good in the presiding chair. The South Carolinian was highly competent and a powerful voice for the Southern constituency. Under Monroe, he had been a very effective secretary of war. Known as the "Young Hercules" of Congress, he was a polished speaker and used his considerable intelligence and powers of persuasion to seek a solution to the problems between North and South. One of his friends found Calhoun so intense that he could only occasionally be in his company, claiming that "when I seek relaxation with him, he screws me only the higher in some sort of excitement"; and another came away muttering, "I hate a man who makes me think so much."

The Jackson–Calhoun partnership was a complete disaster, almost from the beginning. First, there was the Peggy Eaton affair. Calhoun's wife, along with all the other cabinet wives, branded Secretary of War Eaton's wife with an invisible "A" because it was rumored that she had too frequently "left her strait and narrow path." They refused to call on her and snubbed her in general. This infuriated Jackson, who was to have a tantrum or two over the affair. He had another when he discovered that Calhoun, as secretary of war, had once tried to have the then-general Jackson court-martialed for disobeying orders during the War of 1812 and afterward claiming that he would do it again "under the same circumstances." Jackson told Calhoun, "I never expected to say to you . . . Et tu, Brute."

But the main point of contention was Calhoun's firm belief that the states had the right to nullify any federal laws—especially tariffs—they did not like. When his state, South Carolina, voted for such nullification, Jackson threatened to send in the army and then "hang [Calhoun] as high as Haman." A compromise was worked out to avoid this, but even years later Jackson contended that his two main regrets in life were not being able to shoot Henry Clay or to hang Calhoun.

The final straw in Calhoun's frustration with his enforced silence in the Senate chamber may have been the time when a senator criticized him at some length from the floor. The fuming vice-president leaned over to ask: "Does the Senator allude to me?" The senator, knowing the rules, turned to him coldly and asked: "By what right does the Chair ask the question?"

Shortly thereafter, Calhoun leapt at the chance to accept his state's appointment to fill the Senate seat left vacant by Robert Hayne. His resignation gave Calhoun the right to question once more.

Martin Van Buren

"The Little Magician"

DEMOCRATIC-REPUBLICAN
IN OFFICE: 1833–1837
PRESIDENT: ANDREW JACKSON

It is in poor taste to spread rumors, but politicians thrive on them and since all the parties to this one have been dead for many years—and the truth of it could account for many things—it may bear consideration: it was said of Martin Van Buren that he was the bastard son of Aaron Burr. Burr apparently spent some time during the Revolution relaxing at the tavern that Van Buren's father ran in Kinderhook, New York. This happened to be around the time of little Mattie's birth—give or take a few months. John Quincy Adams, in remarking on the rumors in his diary, noted the resemblance between the two men, who in fact became close personal friends; both had slight trim figures, both were dandies, and both were attractive to women.

However it came about, Van Buren had politics in his blood. Before he was old enough to vote, he had success-

MARTIN VAN BUREN
(Artist: Charles Fenderich. National Portrait Gallery, Smithsonian Institution, Washington, D.C.)

fully managed one election campaign. He became a leader in New York City's Tammany Society and was one of the creators of the so-called "Albany regency." He used both political organizations to further his career. One of his cohorts in the latter group, William L. Marcy, coined the phrase—which gave a certain rationale to political patronage—"To the victor belongs the spoils of the enemy!"

The "enemy" was naturally any member of the opposition party, as by this time the two-party system had become well established in American politics. In the election of 1828, the supporters of John Quincy Adams—Northern manufacturers, Antimasons, erstwhile Federalists, and conservative nationalists—called themselves National-Republicans or Whigs. The Democratic-Republicans (soon shortened to Democratics) backed Jackson and consisted of Westerners, small nonslaveholding farmers, the powerful Scotch-Irish contingent, and what is broadly referred to as the "common man." As suffrage was being extended to include nonproperty owners, the electoral system was broadening and becoming more responsive to the voice of the people. The spoils system was a logical way to reward party workers.

Van Buren was dedicated to furthering the aims of his party, the Democratic, and fully expected the party to do the same for him. After ten years as a state senator, he was twice elected to the U.S. Senate. His political maneuverings in the Senate led a colleague to remark that within "two weeks Van Buren will become perfectly acquainted with the views and feelings of every member, yet no man will know his."

It did not require much perspicacity on Van Buren's part to see that Jackson would defeat Adams in 1828, and he set out to make himself an indispensable part of the new administration. While working for Jackson's election in New York, Van Buren also ran for and won the governorship. This was mainly to keep the office from falling into Whig hands, for he counted on being named to a cabinet post once Jackson was elected.

As Jackson's secretary of state, 1829–1831, Van Buren further endeared himself to the president by being kind to the secretary of war's wife, Peggy Eaton, when all Washington was snubbing her. He then hit on the solution to this sticky situation that was creating a rift between president and cabinet by suggesting that the entire cabinet, including himself, resign. That way Jackson would not seem to be giving in to pressure to fire Eaton. A contemporary noted that Van Buren deserved the nickname "Little Magician," because he just "raises his wand and the whole Cabinet vanishes."

Jackson then appointed Van Buren ambassador to Great Britain, and Mattie sailed for London. When the vote for confirmation came up in the Senate, however, his recently acquired enemy, Vice-President Calhoun—who had lost several supporters when the cabinet resigned—saw his chance to inflict a wound, and cast a deciding "Nay" vote against the appointment. Calhoun now thought Van Buren's career was finished, that he would "never kick again." But Missouri senator Thomas Hart Benson took a different view. "You have broken a minister," he told Calhoun, "and elected a vice-president."

Sure enough, the perverse love of Americans for the

underdog gave Van Buren such sympathetic support that he won the Democratic vice-presidential nomination and was elected in 1832. That year also saw the first of the national party conventions that have become the quadrennial productions Americans know and love. The losing Whig ticket was headed by Senator Henry Clay of Kentucky and Pennsylvania congressman John Sergeant.

As vice-president, Van Buren was pretty much of a cipher, sticking to his policy of not offending anyone by a strong stand on anything. His method of presiding was described as "exasperatingly unruffled," although on one occasion he was forced to carry two pistols to defend himself from the ire of Whig senator George Poindexter. Poindexter had challenged Van Buren to a duel for calling him "that bloated mass of corruption"; but the confrontation never came off.

By 1836, the astute little politician was just what he wanted to be: the Democratic candidate for president. The campaign was a particularly dirty one, and Van Buren was smeared himself with some of the mud being slung. Davy Crockett wrote a nastily amusing biography of him, saying in part: ". . . at one year of age he could cry out of one side of his face and laugh out of the other . . . He wears corsets and, if possible, he wears them tighter than the women. He struts and swaggers like a crow in the gutter. But for his large red and gray whiskers it would be difficult to tell whether he was man or woman."

The presidency did not turn out to be the plum Van Buren had anticipated. For one thing, he had for too long "rowed to his object with muffled oars" (as John Randolph said). His vagueness and soft-spokenness had left him somewhat of an enigma to other politicians, who were unsure of whether or not to support him because they did not know where he stood. Also, he had inherited and was blamed for a great depression. Finally, it may be that he had spent so much time and thought on how to get to higher office that he did not know what to do with it once he got there.

Like Calhoun, Van Buren had wanted the vice-presidency for a stepping-stone, and this time the gambit was successful. But it would be the last time anyone would be elected president directly from that office.

Richard Mentor Johnson

"My Dear Colonel"

DEMOCRAT

IN OFFICE: 1837–1841

PRESIDENT: MARTIN VAN BUREN

The personal life of Richard Johnson, the first vice-president to come from a Western state, would almost certainly not survive the close scrutiny of today's mass media. Even with a running mate "1,000 percent" behind him, he would undoubtedly have been disqualified as a vice-presidential candidate on the grounds of offending certain sensibilities. In 1836, most people were not aware of the situation, but his fellow politicians knew that bachelor Johnson kept three black mistresses—though not all at once.

The first, Julia Chinn, a mulatto slave inherited from his father, was the mother of Richard's two daughters, Adaline and Imogene. Beautiful and well educated, they successfully entered society and both married white men. When Julia died, Johnson took a second mistress, who later ran off with an Indian. He brought the third woman

RICHARD M. JOHNSON

(Artist: Charles Fenderich. National Portrait Gallery, Smithsonian Institution, Washington, D.C.)

to Washington with him to act as his hostess, and she was known to address him as "my dear Colonel" at social gatherings.

There was no stopping his nomination for vice-president, however. Johnson had been handpicked by out-going President Jackson, who was in effect dictating the terms of the Democratic campaign. Jackson remembered Johnson as one of the most vocal hawks of the War of 1812 and as a strong defender of his actions in that war. Jackson was also anxious to break up the old New York–Virginia alliance by bringing in the Kentuckian, Johnson, to balance the ticket with New Yorker Van Buren.

Johnson, who liked to brag that he was "born in a cane brake and cradled in a saptrough," was also supposed to appeal to those who found his running mate too much of a dandy. It was thought that he would balance the ticket in terms of valor, since many considered the presidential candidate, Van Buren, a battle-shirker for sitting out the war. The Whigs were offering ex-general William Henry Harrison as their candidate, so it seemed a good idea to have an ex-soldier on the Democratic ticket, too. Johnson was viewed as a genuine American hero because he was the slayer of the great Shawnee Indian chief, Tecumseh. He could not actually prove this—no scalp on his belt or suchlike—but several witnesses backed Johnson up on his account of the fighting at the Battle of the Thames. There were those who argued that a lucky shot did not make him fit for office, but the campaign slogan "Rumpsey Dumpsey, Rumpsey Dumpsey, Colonel Johnson killed Tecumsey" would have a magnetic appeal.

Of course, Johnson was not just plucked from the

battlefield to run for this high political office. For twenty years, he had worked hard in both House and Senate in behalf of a variety of interesting bills. He strongly advocated regular Sunday delivery of mail, claiming the practice of treating the day as a Christian holiday violated the principle of separation of church and state (he also felt that receiving letters from friends was in itself a kind of balm to the spirit). Johnson worked, too, to do away with debtors' prisons and—perhaps because he was not too solvent himself—to increase the pay of legislators. And in spite of, or maybe because of, having killed Tecumseh he wanted to improve the lives of Indians, for he founded the Choctaw Academy to further their education.

It was probably due to his flaunting of his life-style and ignoring Southern mores that he was unable to carry even his own state in the election of 1836. In fact, the election was so close that he missed receiving a majority by one vote. This threw the election into the Senate, and Johnson became the first and only vice-president to be elected in this manner.

As vice-president, he pretty much did what he had to do—broke a few tie votes and kept a little order in the Senate—and still managed to have time to attend to things at the resort he had built on his land at White Sulphur Springs, in what was then Virginia. There guests were amazed to see the vice-president giving his personal attention to "the chicken and egg purchasing and water-melon selling department."

But careless personal habits, added to his other idiosyncrasies, increasingly made Johnson a political liability. One Senate doorkeeper claimed that Johnson was "the most vulgar man of all vulgar men in this world." Eventually even Jackson turned against him and admitted that he should be dropped from the ticket at the next convention, in 1840. The Democrats, unable to resolve the question of a vice-presidential candidate in that year, chose no one at all, leaving it up to individual states to choose their own nominees.

Johnson was not willing to be counted out, however, and vowed to "go into the fight, show my scars and be reelected." He really wanted to serve another term under Van Buren and then to follow him into the White House. And he did get enough states to vote him onto the ticket with Van Buren. But this time it didn't really matter, since the Democrats lost in 1840 by a wide margin.

So Johnson went home to Kentucky. He did not fully relinquish his national ambitions until he had lost the presidential nomination as his state's favorite-son candidate in 1844 and again in 1848. He spent the rest of his life in the Kentucky State Senate, staying well beyond his years of usefulness apparently, for one local newspaper opined: "He is totally unfit for the business of a legislature."

John Tyler

"His Accidency"

WHIG

IN OFFICE: 1841

PRESIDENT:

WILLIAM HENRY HARRISON

Vice-president John Tyler was at his home in Williamsburg, Virginia, when he first heard about the death of President Harrison a month after the inauguration. He had the several hours it took to return to Washington to reflect on his course of action. His decision set the precedent for all future succeeding vice-presidents. The sentence of the Constitution that concerned him read:

> In case of the Removal of the President from Office, or of his Death, Resignation, or Inability to discharge the Powers and Duties of said Office, the same shall devolve on the Vice President . . .

For the first time in the nation's history, it had to be decided whether the authors of the Constitution (not one of whom was around to clarify the situation) intended for the vice-president to assume merely the powers and duties of the presidency, or the office itself. Tyler decided not to spend the next four years as acting-president. He took the oath of office as president.

John Quincy Adams, as acerbic as his father had been, expressed the feelings of the many critics of this action when he wrote that "His Accidency" Tyler "styles himself President of the United States, and not vice-president acting as President, which would be the correct style." Tyler, he went on, had "talents not above mediocrity, and a spirit incapable of expansion to the dimensions of the station upon which he has been cast," and said that Harrison's death had put in the executive's seat "a man never thought of for it by anybody."

Tyler had become vice-president in one of the most strident campaigns ever conducted. By 1840, the American people were rapidly spreading out across the Midwest and there had already surfaced feelings of inferiority to and resentment of the Eastern establishment. Andrew Jackson had been the first champion of this new bloc of voters. Smart politicians in the Whig party knew that William Henry Harrison, another general with a background of War of 1812 victories similar to Jackson's, could win this time—he had lost in 1836—and they could oust Van Buren from the White House.

Harrison, a sixty-eight-year-old former general and the hero of the Battle of Tippecanoe, came from Southern aristocracy and lived in a sixteen-room mansion, but he coyly called it his "log cabin at the Bend" and voters took him at his word. Certainly he was humble in political experience; although he had once briefly served as House member and ambassador, his job prior to the

JOHN TYLER

(Artist: George Peter Alexander Healy. National Portrait Gallery, Smithsonian Institution, Washington, D.C.)

election was clerk of the Court of Common Pleas of Hamilton County, Ohio. Powerful Whigs such as Henry Clay and Daniel Webster, who were too controversial to win an election themselves, were confident of having things their way with such a political nonentity in office. Nicholas Biddle, who ran the campaign, let it be known that he told Harrison to allow no one to "ever extract from him a single word, about what he thinks now, or what he will do hereafter."

The campaign depended on songs and doggerel to sway public opinion. One favorite went

Old Tip he wears a homespun suit,
He has no ruffled shirt—wirt, wirt;
But Mat he has the golden plate,
And he's a little squirt—wirt, wirt.

(It was best to sing this outdoors, because the men were supposed to spit everytime they said "wirt.") Another popular ditty in favor of Harrison, the "log cabin" candidate, was:

Let Van from his coolers of silver drink wine,
And lounge on his cushioned settee;
Our man on his buckeye bench can recline,
Content with hard cider is he!

Virginia aristocrat John Tyler had been hoping to return to the Senate seat he had resigned four years earlier in a dispute with President Jackson over the National Bank Bill. However, like others in love or politics who leave the scene for too long, he found that his place had been taken by another. He was offered the vice-presidency nomination as consolation.

Tyler sat out most of the campaign to avoid revealing his strong views and the fact that he did not have a log cabin. When he did appear in public, he referred all questions to his record. If anyone had bothered to check, it might have been discovered that his un-Whiglike views on tariffs and banking and his strong pro-states' rights stand were much too rigid to suit those who were planning to control the government.

The Whigs rode the catchy slogan "Tippecanoe and Tyler Too" into power in Washington, but Harrison's sudden death made many regret the line. New York Whig Philip Hone said, "Poor Tippecanoe! It was an evil hour that 'Tyler Too' was added to make out the line. There was rhyme but no reason to it." Just one month after his inauguration, President Harrison, though certainly not opposed to the political spoils system, began to find the pressure of importuning office seekers more than he could stand. He complained that he had no time even for "the necessary functions of nature." Finally, when he could stand their clamoring no longer, he fled into the cold rainy night, caught pneumonia, and died.

The problems of the Whigs' supposed "balanced" ticket soon began to reveal themselves. Tyler would not agree to let policy be decided by a cabinet vote with the president having only one equal vote, as Harrison had done. Within months, the entire cabinet resigned except for Secretary of State Daniel Webster. When Tyler began to veto bills, such as that for forming a national bank, proposed by the Whigs, he was ousted from the party. He became our only president without a party.

The turnover rate of his cabinet set a record, with three attorneys general, five secretaries of war, five secretaries of the navy, four secretaries of the treasury, two postmasters general and four secretaries of state. All in just one term. Congress threatened impeachment of Tyler but failed to get the necessary votes. One editor claimed that the attempt failed so that Tyler would not be made a martyr, which "might invest nothingness with consequence."

Tyler's troubled presidency was not without its personal pleasures. He married for a second time—a woman thirty years younger than himself—and raised a total of fifteen children. Obviously washed up in national politics after 1844, the ex-president returned to his beloved South. He was a member of the Congress of the Confederate States of America when he died.

Teddy Roosevelt later expressed the opinion of many when he called Tyler "a politician of monumental littleness."

George Mifflin Dallas

The Last Pennsylvanian

DEMOCRAT
IN OFFICE: 1845–1849
PRESIDENT: JAMES K. POLK

One might assume that after the Tyler debacle, politicians would think twice about choosing a vice-president with different views from those of the presidential nominee. But the Democrats in 1844 did not seem to have learned that lesson. Their first choice for the number-two spot was Senator Silas Wright of New York. He was directly opposed to the stand of presidential nominee James Knox Polk on the most pressing question of the time: the annexation of Texas.

As Wright did not attend the convention in Baltimore, the vice-presidential offer was made by telegraph—a modern miracle at the time—and it was refused by the same means. When Wright turned down the offer a second time, the assumption was that the newly invented machine had gone awry. A delegation from the convention rushed to Washington to hear Wright's answer in the old-fashioned way—face to face—and to their dismay found that the telegraph did indeed work.

Wright would not run because the ticket did not include his friend Van Buren, who had wanted a second term but ruined his chances by opposing the annexation of Texas. When Van Buren could not get the two-thirds vote necessary for nomination, it slipped away from him on the ninth ballot and into the lap of "dark horse" Polk. Polk, onetime Speaker of the House and governor of Tennessee, had been hanging around the convention figuring to win, perhaps, the vice-presidency.

By the time the presidential nomination was settled, the convention seemed to have been going on forever. The delegates quickly and gratefully accepted the suggestion of Mississippi senator Robert J. Walker that his brother-in-law, George Dallas from Pennsylvania, be the nominee for vice-president. Dallas was somewhat of a political anomaly; he enjoyed politics and diplomacy but was not consumed by ambition for ever-higher office. Up to the time of the convention his career had included a time as mayor of Philadelphia, as U.S. district attorney, briefly in a fill-in capacity as U.S. senator, and as minister to Russia. In Moscow he became quite friendly with Tsar Nicholas but found the assignment somewhat unnecessary, saw no reason "in even being there"—and asked to come home after two years.

The campaign of 1844 was fairly mild compared with the slogans and singing hysteria of four years before. The Whigs' slogan, "The country's risin'/For Clay and Frelinghuysen," not surprisingly never caught on. The Democrats used "Polk, Dallas and Texas," which was not catchy but contained all the important elements.

GEORGE M. DALLAS

(Artist: A. Hoffy. Collections of the Library of Congress)

Just before election day, a New York newspaper printed an account of Polk purchasing and branding his initials on several slaves, as witnessed by a Baron Roorback. Several other Whig journals printed the story before it was proven to be a complete fabrication, but by then it was too late for disclaimers. It did not prove lethal to Polk's campaign, but it did add a new word to the political lexicon: "the Roorback." This ploy of giving out a damaging story too close to election to be disproved has, of course, been used rather frequently ever since.

Some exciting events took place during Dallas's term as vice-president, most of them related to the great geographical expansion that the nation referred to as its Manifest Destiny. The town and county of Dallas, Texas, founded in 1846, were named in honor of the incumbent vice-president. There was a war with Mexico, the Oregon boundary dispute was settled with Great Britain, and California became a U.S. territory and hosted a great gold rush.

During his tenure, Dallas did what was necessary on the job and got along very well with Polk, whose determination to serve only one term did not seem to afflict Dallas with high presidential fever. In fact, his loyalty to Polk was probably his political downfall. Dallas incurred the wrath of Pennsylvania protectionists by casting the tie-breaking vote in favor of Polk's low-tariff bill, even though opposed to it himself. Pennsylvanians were so angry that Dallas felt it necessary to write home, telling his wife to "pack up and bring the whole brood to Washington" and, presumably, safety. Newspaper editorials in the state went so far as to curse all future vice-presidents from Pennsylvania, saying, "We have had enough of one to last us while all who live now shall continue to breathe . . ." This is apparently still true, since Dallas was the last vice-president from that state.

In an apparent attempt to rationalize the need for and the prestige of the vice-presidency, Dallas once wrote that in the first place the "incumbent is anointed by the national ballot-box, second, its action is manifested in the noblest of all deliberative bodies, the Senate of the U.S., and third, its *accidency* is the supreme executive."

Millard Fillmore

Last Whig, First "Know-Nothing"

WHIG

IN OFFICE: 1849–1850

PRESIDENT: ZACHARY TAYLOR

There is in Buffalo, New York, near Millard Fillmore's birthplace, an organization called the Millard Fillmore Society. It consists of three members: two humans and a dog. The other known Fillmore Society is located in Cascade, Colorado. Its members call themselves "Fill-morons." This may suggest a lot about our twelfth vice-president and thirteenth president—but not everything.

Fillmore came from a family of dirt-poor farmers in upstate New York. When things became really rough, he was apprenticed to a wool carder, with whom he stayed for five years. His education was spotty, but he managed to read for the law and eventually set up a practice in Buffalo. It was at about this time that he met the two men who would infect him with political fever: Thurlow Weed and William H. Seward. Newspaper publisher Weed was the Whig power broker in New York

MILLARD FILLMORE
(Artist: Adam Weingartner. National Portrait Gallery, Smithsonian Institution, Washington, D.C.)

State and Seward was his protégé. They gave the ambitious Fillmore his start by helping to elect him to the state legislature and then to the U.S. Congress, but drew the line at giving him the governorship. Fillmore had to settle for the office of state comptroller, to which he was elected in 1847. From this relatively lowly post he would vault into the presidency.

At the Whig convention of 1848, Henry Clay was again denied a nomination for president. His strong and controversial personality was bypassed in favor of the fourth illustrious general to whet the continuing appetite of party politicians for former military leaders: Zachary Taylor. "Old Rough-and-Ready" was the hero of the Battle of Buena Vista in the Mexican War. Although he admitted to never having voted and to lacking a strong party affiliation, Taylor felt that he was a Whig "but not ultra-Whig" and that that was good enough for him to receive the party's nomination.

Embittered Clay backers were allowed to pick the man for second place, and they looked to New York for someone to "balance" the ticket with Louisianian Taylor. They might not even have noticed Fillmore except that his name was placed in nomination by a fellow New Yorker who was simply trying to make sure he would not have competition for the New York Senate seat he coveted. Michigan senator Lewis Cass and General William O. Butler of Kentucky were nominated by the Democrats.

Following the election, Fillmore began his term high in President Taylor's favor, but he was soon overshadowed by Senator Seward of the old Weed–Seward–Fillmore axis. Now, however, Weed and Seward were on the outs with Fillmore, and the more powerful, Seward, gained control of all of New York's political patronage. One pro-Seward paper claimed, "We could put up a cow against a Fillmore nominee and defeat him." Seward himself felt that Fillmore was "too dull of comprehension really to understand what has happened."

President Taylor was providing a few surprises of his own, once in office. Accustomed to command, he was not pliable enough for some of his wily backers, and fellow Southerners were dismayed by what they saw as his betrayal of them on the issue of slavery.

Slavery was *the* issue in that Senate over which Fillmore presided. Northern abolitionists nearly came to blows several times with Southern supporters of the so-called "peculiar institution." There were new territories in the West, and the Senate had to decide whether they would eventually join the Union as free or slave states. President Taylor, although a slaveholder himself, felt that national unity was more important than sectional rivalry. He pushed to bring California into the union without its first serving time as a territory, knowing that California would choose to enter as a free state. This would eliminate rancorous Senate debate on its statehood. The South was incensed by the plan, and the Civil War might have begun ten years early had it not been for the Compromise Plan of 1850 arranged by Henry Clay. One part of this compromise was the inclusion of California in the Union as a free state; another was the obliging of the Northern states to return fugitive slaves to their "owners."

Because of this last part of the compromise, Taylor

would not go along with it, and Seward acted as his spokesman in the Senate. A desire to oppose anything that Seward now championed may have influenced Fillmore's decision to vote *for* the compromise. In any case, he informed the president that he would do so if, as was likely, the Senate became deadlocked on the plan.

A few days later, on the Fourth of July, 1850, President Taylor presided over the laying of the Washington Monument cornerstone. Sitting in the hot sun, he drank several glasses of water, and on his return to the White House ate cherries with cold milk. This sounds innocent enough, but Taylor came down with what his doctors called "cholera morbus" and five days later was dead.

Much to the chagrin of fellow New Yorkers Seward and Weed, Fillmore was now in, and so was the Compromise of 1850. Fillmore's support of the Fugitive Slave Act led to his being termed a "Doughface," a strange name coined by John Randolph at the time of the Missouri Compromise (1820) to identify Northerners who entertained Southern views on slavery. It also ruined his chances in the North for nomination as president in 1852. The Whigs nominated yet another Mexican War general, Winfield Scott (who lost). But by this time the Whig party was nearly defunct. There were too many opposing factions within its ranks, and its two strongest leaders, Clay and Webster, died in 1852.

Millard Fillmore still wanted to be president in his own right, and in 1856 he headed the Know-Nothing ticket. This splinter party came into being in response to fears that immigrants and Catholics were going to take over the government. Party members were told to respond simply that they "know nothing," to all questions about their ultraconservative views. Although 21 percent of the voters seemed to agree with this "America for Americans" stand, they were not enough to put Fillmore back in office.

William Rufus DeVane King

"Miss Nancy"

DEMOCRAT

IN OFFICE: 1853

PRESIDENT: FRANKLIN PIERCE

If William Rufus DeVane King is remembered today—and it would be no great slur on anyone's pretensions to historical knowledge not to know of him—it is probably as the vice-president who never served, and who helped to create a vice-presidential vacuum that lasted for several years. King died before taking office and was in fact known to be terminally ill with tuberculosis when nominated. This raises some interesting questions about the motives of the Democrats, who selected him. Perhaps it was an attempt on their part to sober up the presidential nominee, Franklin Pierce, whom one Whig punster characterized as "a hero of many a well-fought bottle."

King was not a memorable politician in spite of the fact that he had served in the Senate for nearly thirty years. Elected to the House when he was just twenty-four, he

WILLIAM RUFUS DEVANE KING
(Artist: Charles Fenderich. National Portrait Gallery, Smithsonian Institution, Washington, D.C.)

was also one of Alabama's first senators, though "not particularly able" (according to John Calhoun). He served as president pro tem of the Senate on several occasions, including the period when Fillmore succeeded to the presidency, and was ambassador to France under Presidents Tyler and Polk.

The vice-presidency seems to have been his ambition for a long while, and his name had been mentioned several times before 1852. In that year he was finally chosen to "balance" the ticket with dark-horse candidate Pierce, a New Hampshire man with little political experience. Inexperience was considered an advantage in this time of so much contention over the slavery issue: it gave the opposition little to criticize. The rather peculiar campaign slogan was "We Polked you in 1844, we shall Pierce you in 1852!" As it turned out, Pierce was a weak, vacillating leader—another "Doughface" president, who promised that there would be no more "agitation of the slavery question" and whose secretary of war was the future president of the Confederacy, Jefferson Davis.

If King had lived, the retiring little man would have presided over a raucous Senate filled with portents of violence. Senator Stephen Douglas of Illinois pushed through his Kansas-Nebraska Act in 1854. This act gave the people rather than Congress the right to decide whether a state would be slave or free, and repealed a law that had prohibited slavery north of a certain latitude. Anti-slavery Northerners, outraged at the repeal, formed the Republican party in response.

King also would have witnessed an attack on Massachusetts senator Charles Sumner by South Carolina congressman Preston Brooks. Brooks, outraged by Sumner's "slavery is a harlot" speech, beat him over the head with a cane in the Senate chambers. Sumner did not recover for three years, and Brooks was fined three hundred dollars.

Opposition party members gossiped about the relationship between King and politician James Buchanan. The two bachelors shared an apartment in Washington, and King was known to write rather gushing letters to Buchanan when the two were separated. Andrew Jackson had referred to King as "Miss Nancy"; John Quincy Adams called him a "gentle slave-monger"—whatever that might intimate. Just about everyone ridiculed him for wearing a wig when they were long out of fashion.

When the call to the vice-presidency came, King, desperately ill, had gone to Cuba for medical treatment. He was given special permission by Congress to take the oath of office in Havana but was so weak he had to be propped up by aides for the swearing in. Realizing that the end was near, he insisted that he be allowed to go back to his home in Alabama to die. And that is what he did, shortly after his return.

Fellow senators found it difficult to eulogize the man. Once mention had been made of King's long years of service, there was not much to add. Journalist Nathan Sargent remembered him as that "nice, natty gentleman very tenacious of the observance of etiquette." Others, who really tried, came up with the "kindliness of spirit" and "gracious manner" of the "quiet and meek Mr. King."

John Cabell Breckinridge

Kentuckian with a Silver Tongue

DEMOCRAT
IN OFFICE: 1857–1861
PRESIDENT: JAMES BUCHANAN

John Breckinridge became our second and last (to date) vice-president to be accused of treason, joining the colorful company of Aaron Burr. Unlike Burr, however, Breckinridge was never brought to trial.

If Breckinridge were alive today, when charisma really counts for something, or if charisma had been *the* political quality to have in the mid-1800s, he might well have become our youngest president. As it was, he was our youngest vice-president at thirty-six. Of course, after the nation's brief experience with King, even an uncharismatic person would probably have been chosen, as long as he was young and healthy.

Breckinridge was an outstanding orator and, when oiled with some of his native Kentucky's favorite beverage, could be absolutely spellbinding. As a thirty-year-old Democrat, he managed to win a House seat from a

JOHN C. BRECKINRIDGE
(National Portrait Gallery, Smithsonian Institution, Washington, D.C.)

strongly Whig district. When fellow-Kentuckian Henry Clay died, Breckinridge was chosen to give the eulogy, and he did so, brilliantly. Unfortunately, the times were not propitious for a Southern leader on the national scene, and his political career was finished before he was fifty.

In 1856, to please the Southern Democrats, Breckinridge was nominated to run with James Buchanan of Pennsylvania. Buchanan was elderly but had one glowing recommendation for election: he had been out of the country, serving as minister to Great Britain, at the time of the passage of the Kansas-Nebraska Act, a period that had sullied so many political reputations. His heart was not completely in the race, though: the troubled times would have been difficult for almost any leader, and Buchanan felt too tired for the challenge. Also, he mused, "I am too old, my friends are all gone, I have no one to reward; my enemies are dead, I have no one to gloat over."

The Democrats won in a close contest against the new Republican party headed by California "Pathfinder" John Frémont and the Know-Nothings headed by Millard Fillmore. Buchanan became the last of the "Doughface" presidents, preferring the gentle ways of the Southern aristocracy to the rowdy manners of the abolitionists, and taking no moral stand against slavery.

As vice-president, Breckinridge was well liked and considered fair by both parties. In his home state, he was so popular that he was elected to the Senate two years before his term as vice-president was up. Kentuckians knew they wanted him to represent them "if and when he is no longer vice-president."

During the four years of Breckinridge's vice-presidency, the nation moved inexorably toward civil war. The Dred Scott decision of 1857, handed down by Chief Justice Roger B. Taney, declared that the black race "had no rights which the white man was bound to respect," that slaves were "articles of merchandise," and that Congress could not pass legislation against slavery. This frightened and angered the free states, turning many previously undecided voters against the South and the Democrats. Two years later, John Brown was hanged for leading the abortive slave insurrection at Harper's Ferry, Virginia, and became a folk hero in the North.

By 1860, the Democrats themselves were split into Northern and Southern factions. Stephen Douglas was nominated to head the Northern ticket, while Breckinridge was talked into running for president by the Southerners. Democratic divisiveness insured a win for the Republicans' Abraham Lincoln, but Breckinridge still had his senatorial position waiting, so it was not a complete loss for him.

As senator, Breckinridge wanted to preserve the Union but he also believed in the right of individual states to secede. Douglas noted: "Breckinridge may not be for disunion but all the disunionists are for Breckinridge." In one of his stirring speeches, Breckinridge urged Kentucky to remain neutral in the coming civil conflict. Kentucky followed his advice, but when Union troops moved in and took control, the state had to ask him to resign from the Senate. Soon after, Breckinridge fled to the South to join the Confederate Army. He claimed that he had exchanged "with satisfaction a term of six years in the Senate for the musket of a soldier." He saw action in many of the well-known battles of the Civil War and rose to the rank of major general. In 1865, he was appointed Confederate president Jefferson Davis's secretary of war.

It was these actions that led to his being indicted for treason. The fact that he had joined the Rebels even though his state had not seceded meant that he would be dealt with quite harshly at war's end, so he opted for discretion finally and fled the country. With a band of faithful followers, he made his way through the South and then across to Cuba. For the next four years, Breckinridge and his family roamed through England, Europe, and Canada, supported by Southern and English sympathizers. He was eventually allowed to come home in 1868 under the terms of President Andrew Johnson's general amnesty, and received a hero's welcome in Lexington, Kentucky. As one observer noted, "Kentucky did not join the Confederacy until after the war." In any case, it was not until 1958 that Kentucky courts dismissed the charges of treason against one of their favorite sons.

Hannibal Hamlin

"The Most Unimportant Man in Washington"

REPUBLICAN

IN OFFICE: 1861–1865

PRESIDENT: ABRAHAM LINCOLN

Hannibal Hamlin's name has a nice alliterative ring, and today's public relations people might have done wonders with it. In 1860, they only came up with "Abra*Ham*-Lincoln"—pretty clever, but how do you say it?

Hamlin was not, of course, nominated to run with Lincoln because of his name. Coming from Maine, he "balanced" the Republican ticket led by a man from the West (Illinois). And he was acceptable to New York senator William H. Seward's supporters, who had tried but failed to put their man in the top spot. Hamlin also had the necessary antislavery, pro-Union views, although because of his own dark complexion, he was accused of having Negro blood. Trying to be humorous, three Southerners once offered to buy him from Lincoln as a slave.

Hamlin had also paid his political dues. Unable to

afford college, he had been a farmer for a time before obtaining his law degree. It may be that there is a subliminal message in law books about the rewards of a political career, because, as so often happens to law school graduates, politics beckoned Hamlin. He was elected to the House of Representatives and then the Senate. He resigned from the Senate to run for Maine governor. He resigned as governor (after a month) to run again for the Senate. Somewhere along this hectic route, he switched from the Democratic to the Republican party. Hamlin was clearly an opportunist.

He was also a strong advocate of patronage. In fact, one of his biggest disappointments in the vice-presidency was its remove from the spoils system. He felt powerless in other ways too, telling one petitioner, "I am not consulted at all, nor do I think there is much disposition . . . to regard any counsel I may give." He moaned that he was "the most unimportant man in Washington, ignored by the President, the Cabinet, and Congress."

Lincoln did not know Hamlin very well; they did not meet until after the nominations. This situation was becoming the norm rather than the exception; as the country grew, and with it the number of political aspirants, it simply became more and more difficult for party hopefuls to know everyone. Following his nomination, Hamlin wrote Lincoln that he would like to become "intimately acquainted in the coming four years." But Lincoln would have more on his mind than making friends with his vice-president. Before he was even inaugurated, seven states seceded to form the Confederate States of America.

Lincoln did set Hamlin one delicate task in the course

HANNIBAL HAMLIN
(Photographer: Mathew Brady. Collections of the Library of Congress)

of forming his cabinet. Lincoln did not want Senator Seward in his administration. He had been assured that Seward would refuse any offer, but that an invitation of some kind would be an important boost to party unity. So Hamlin was sent to offer Seward, strictly as a gesture of solidarity, the position of secretary of state. Hamlin was chagrined and Lincoln was angry when Seward (who was probably amused) accepted.

As vice-president, Hamlin spent very little time in the capital, letting a president pro tempore preside in his place as he went on his frequent trips to Maine. But he did accomplish some things while in office. He successfully pushed for the enlistment of blacks in the army, and he forbade the sale of liquor in the Senate chambers. And either boredom with the vice-presidency or patriotism in time of war prompted Hamlin to enlist in the Maine Coast Guard, where he served as a private for sixty days.

Whether or not he enjoyed the vice-presidency, Hamlin had expected to be offered a second term and was disappointed that Andrew Johnson was named to run with Lincoln instead. It appears that Hamlin was so unpopular with some people that, as one editor put it, Lincoln might be killed except "that Hamlin is a bigger fool than he is." Also, by 1864, the North seemed to be winning the war, and Republicans felt the need to look farther south than New England for a running mate. Furthermore, Lincoln considered Hamlin's views on Reconstruction of the postwar South too severe. So when the president informed the 1864 convention that it "must judge for itself" on the vice-president, that was translated to mean that Hamlin was out.

In the long run, it may have been the best thing for Hamlin. He was reelected to the Senate in 1868 and returned to what he liked best—handing out political plums—for the next twelve years. Later, to satisfy his desire to travel, he requested a diplomatic post and was named minister to Spain. He died on July 4, 1891, the third vice-president (along with Adams and Jefferson) to die on Independence Day.

Andrew Johnson

War Democrat from Tennessee

DEMOCRAT
IN OFFICE: 1865
PRESIDENT: ABRAHAM LINCOLN

O, was it not a glorious sight,
To see the crowd of black and white,
As well as Andy Johnson tight
At the inauguration.

Seeing the new vice-president "tight" at his inauguration may have given perverse pleasure to Andrew Johnson's enemies, but it was not a glorious start for the second Lincoln administration.

Before outgoing vice-president Hannibal Hamlin could administer the oath of office, Johnson leapt to the podium and delivered a long, rambling harangue that caused Lincoln to lower his eyes in embarrassment and weaker men to hide their heads in their desks. Waving his arms and raising his voice, Johnson admonished the senators to remember their debt to the common men who

ANDREW JOHNSON
(Artists: Currier and Ives. National Portrait Gallery, Smithsonian Institution, Washington, D.C.)

had put them in office—a speech hard to take even for those naive enough to believe it. He then took the oath and would have launched into a second oration if he had not been physically restrained by those around him. (Charles Dickens once described Johnson's face as that of a man who could not "be turned or trifled with. A man [I should say] who would have to be killed to be got out of the way.")

It would, however, be unjust to permit this usually abstemious man to go down in history as a lush or, as Navy Secretary Gideon Welles said, "deranged." There were extenuating circumstances. Recovering from a bout of typhoid fever, Johnson had wanted to take the oath of office in Nashville. Lincoln insisted he come to Washington, wiring Johnson that "it is unsafe for you not to be here on the 4th of March." Johnson arrived at the capital in time for a stag party on the eve of the inauguration, and the next morning, weak from fever, hung over and nervous, in Hamlin's overheated office he waited for the ceremonies to begin. There are those who say it was the vengeance of a rejected man that made Hamlin offer Johnson several glasses of brandy to settle his nerves, but this implies a degree of vindictiveness hard to believe. Prophetic critics railed that "only one frail life stands between this insolent, clownish drunk and the Presidency." But Lincoln stood up for the number-two man, calling the incident "a bad slip" and proclaiming, "Andy ain't a drunkard." He admired Johnson's courage, and claimed the Tennessean was "too much of a man for the American people to cast him off for a single error."

Lincoln found much to admire in Andrew Johnson, including the fact that as a war Democrat from Tennessee he would bring in needed votes from Democrats in the North and in the border states. Pennsylvania Representative Thaddeus Stevens complained that the Republican convention should have been able to find a candidate "without going down into a damned rebel province for one." Democratic newspapers thought Lincoln and Johnson deserved each other; the New York *World* wrote that they were a "railsplitting buffoon and a boorish tailor . . . men of mediocre talents, narrow views, deficient education and coarse, vulgar manners" and, furthermore, "two ignorant, boorish, third-rate backwoods lawyers." Union victories in the field contributed to the overwhelming Republican defeat of the Democrat candidates, General George B. McClellan and Ohio congressman George H. Pendleton.

North Carolinian by birth, Johnson had been apprenticed to a tailor when he was fourteen and taught himself to read and write with the help of his wife. By the time he was twenty, and settled in Tennessee, he was elected to the town council, and he rose to become congressman, then governor of Tennessee, and then senator, 1857–1862. He was the only senator from a Confederate state to remain in the U.S. Senate, and was rewarded for his courage by being made the military governor of the state when the Union Army took it over in 1862.

Johnson might have been the first recorded victim of an assassination plot on a vice-president, but he was fortunate in the assassin: George Atzerodt, assigned to Johnson by John Wilkes Booth. Atzerodt had taken a room in Kirkwood House, the Washington hotel where Johnson was staying, April 14, 1865. After checking in,

Atzerodt hid his weapons under his pillow and went out for a drink. This apparently was not enough to bolster his courage, however, and he never returned to carry out his plan to shoot the vice-president in his room. The change of heart saved Johnson's life but could not keep Atzerodt from being hanged.

In a natural American leap of logic, Johnson was suspected of complicity in Lincoln's death on April 15, 1865. His turning down an invitation to Ford's Theatre the night before—calling it a "frivolity"—became suspicious. The about-face of his would-be assassin was suspicious. In Mary Todd Lincoln's mind, everything Johnson did was suspicious.

Johnson's presidency was troubled from the beginning, primarily because of his disagreement with the Radical Republicans, who wanted to punish the Confederate states more than Lincoln and Johnson had thought necessary. Senate Radicals overruled Johnson's vetoes on Reconstruction bills and passed legislation forbidding him from firing the cabinet he had inherited. When Johnson dismissed Secretary of War Edwin Stanton (who had refused to resign and locked himself in his office), the Senate was sure it had grounds for impeachment—better grounds than those once suggested, of insanity or whisky.

Charged with "high crimes and misdemeanors," Johnson was our only president to be impeached and, if he had been convicted, the reverberations might still be felt in the ongoing power struggle between the executive and legislative branches of the U.S. government. Seven Republican senators sacrificed their careers to vote in

Johnson's favor, and the two-thirds vote necessary for conviction failed by one.

Johnson was too controversial to be considered a serious contender in the 1868 presidential election, but six years after leaving office he was once again elected to the Senate. By then, the passionate animosities had faded, and Senator Johnson was greeted in the Senate chamber with applause and with flowers on his desk.

Schuyler Colfax

"The Great Joiner"

REPUBLICAN

IN OFFICE: 1869–1873

PRESIDENT: ULYSSES S. GRANT

In 1868, the vice-presidency started to look amazingly good to a lot of people. After all, if a backwoodsman like Andrew Johnson could make it to the presidency, there was hope for others. The field of contenders was large, though Secretary of the Navy Gideon Welles considered that they were all "very common men, with no decent pretensions to the second position in the Government."

One strong and ambitious aspirant was Schuyler Colfax, a man with two nicknames: "The Smiler" and "The Great Joiner." The first is self-explanatory; he had a face that seemed to have a perpetual grin plastered on it. Welles wrote of Colfax's "heartless everlasting smile and slender abilities"; Lincoln called him a "friendly rascal" and considered him a "little intriguer . . . aspiring beyond his capacity." Colfax's second monicker was a re-

SCHUYLER COLFAX
(Photographers: Mathew Brady and Levin Handy. Collections of the Library of Congress)

flection of his political style: if there was an organization open to new members, Colfax would join it. He probably knew more secret handshakes than any other politician of the time. He even joined the Know-Nothings at their 1855 national convention, though he later contended, in an amazing admission of political blackout, that he "had no knowledge of his election as a delegate."

Smiler grew up in Indiana, where he studied law but never passed the bar. He also owned and edited the St. Joseph Valley *Register* newspaper, a Whig instrument, which endeared him to fellow journalists until he reached such high office that he considered it beneath him to associate with newspaper men. He would soon learn the wrath of the media when spurned.

Present at the creation of the Republican party, he was elected to Congress in 1854 as a Republican and served fourteen years there with three terms as Speaker of the House. There is no record of any effective legislation sponsored by him in that time. He was appointed chairman of the House's Post Offices and Post Roads Committee—a position of some power that, it was later proved, he used to effect bribes.

The Smiler's friends and legions of fellow club members successfully pushed their man as the running mate for Union hero Ulysses S. Grant, even though, for the first time in electoral history, the candidates were from contiguous states: Illinois and Indiana. One Republican leader justified his choice of Colfax by saying, "His abilities are not distinguished but are just sufficient to make him acceptable to the masses. They are fond of happy mediocrity." One newspaper, in describing the differences between the two candidates, noted that it "would be easy to tell from their faces which is the soldier and which is the civilian. Grant's face is fixed and intense in its open firmness and reserve, while Colfax has an amiable countenance, and is a constant and rapid talker." Whatever their facial expressions, Grant and Colfax easily defeated the Democrats, New York governor Horatio Seymour and Missouri politician Francis P. Blair.

Once in office, even Colfax's smile could not hide from Grant the fact that the vice-president now wished to be president. In an attempt to keep him from breathing too heavily down his neck, Grant offered Smiler the position of secretary of state, which Colfax refused because the vice-presidency seemed to offer a better starting gate for first place. When Colfax became convinced that Grant would not seek a second term, he too announced his intention to step down in 1873. This set the stage for Colfax's backers to nominate him for president. Unfortunately for the Smiler, Grant did decide to run again and, although Colfax scrambled to jump back in, it was too late. A replacement vice-president was chosen.

This was just as well, for the discovery of Colfax's involvement in the Crédit Mobilier scandal might have resulted in his impeachment if his term had not been almost over. The scandal originated when Congress agreed to appropriate public funds to supplement private capital for the construction of the Union Pacific Railroad. But the congressmen voted to give much more money than was necessary for the project. Massachusetts congressman Oakes Ames, who was also a director of the railroad, set up the Crédit Mobilier of America and planned to keep the more than $20,000,000 in overfunding. When fellow congressmen became suspicious and threatened an investigation, Ames began selling shares at greatly reduced rates "where [he said] they will do the most good." Colfax received twenty shares.

The vice-president denied any wrongdoing, but a congressional report on his testimony about the charges found it "impossible to believe." His story about a one-thousand-dollar bill unaccountably falling out of an unmarked envelope at his breakfast table was difficult even for hardened politicians to swallow. He used the same rationale to avoid impeachment that Spiro Agnew would resort to one hundred years later; namely, that since the alleged crimes had taken place before he entered office as vice-president, he could not be removed from office for them.

His political career at an end, Colfax joined the lecture circuit, traveling around the country making speeches about Lincoln and about temperance. He died in the course of one such tour, in 1885, in Minnesota, after switching trains in subzero weather. It was said that the Smiler, true to the end, expired with a grin frozen on his face.

Henry Wilson

"The Natick Cobbler"

REPUBLICAN
IN OFFICE: 1873–1875
PRESIDENT: ULYSSES S. GRANT

Henry Wilson changed his name when he turned twenty-one, for reasons that, if they were ever known, are now buried with him. He was born Jeremiah Jones Colbath, a name not without dignity and much more memorable than Henry Wilson. Relabeling himself might have been an attempt to make a complete break with a youth that had been harsh in the extreme.

The son of a large, impoverished Massachusetts family, Wilson was indentured to a farmer when he was ten years old and stayed in this man's custody for eleven years, working in the fields for his room and board. There was no time for school, but Wilson learned to read and devoured hundreds of books. When he left the farm, he had only a few sheep and a pair of oxen, but was apparently sick of dumb animals, so he sold them for eighty-five dollars and signed on as an apprentice to a shoe-

HENRY WILSON
(National Portrait Gallery, Smithsonian Institution, Washington, D.C.)

maker. Six years later, the plucky lad had a prosperous shoe factory of his own. Thus his nickname, "The Natick Cobbler."

Wilson began his political career in the Massachusetts legislature and progressed to the U.S. Senate, where he served for eighteen years. A small, nondescript figure, he did not exactly inspire the masses with his oratory, but he had another technique, which was effective on a smaller scale: by asking the opinions of people he met in the streets or saloons and, later, in the Senate (he may have been the original poll taker), he made them feel that he attached some importance to what they said and that he would act on it. Somewhere in his reading he had apparently learned the importance of flattery.

The two causes dearest to his heart were the abolition of slavery and the amelioration of working conditions for factory employees. He helped to reduce the standard work day from twelve to eight hours and to institute collective bargaining as a means for solving labor-management disputes—which made him unpopular with industrialists. And Southerners resented his antislavery stand so much that, at one period, he took to carrying a couple of pistols for protection from their wrath.

Before the beginning of his senatorial career, Wilson was briefly a Whig, but he deserted that party because of its stand on the slavery question. After a brief and regrettable flirtation with the Know-Nothings, he became a Republican and was appointed chairman of the Military Affairs Committee during the Civil War. One of the Radical Republicans, he pushed for the impeachment of President Andrew Johnson after the war. During the postwar Reconstruction period, Wilson spent some time in North Carolina working with blacks and helping to establish a state Republican party. He also took part in the indictment of some three hundred members of the Ku Klux Klan, which had sprung up since the war.

Wilson won the nomination for vice-president for Grant's second term because he provided a better geographical "balance" for the ticket and was less offensive personally than his predecessor. Although involved in the same Crédit Mobilier scandal that had ruined Colfax, Wilson's claim that he had returned his twenty shares shortly after receiving them convinced the investigating committee that his sins were not beyond what was acceptable for a politician. He was not completely cleared until after the election, but since Grant's reelection was assured, this did not matter.

The graft in high places that was so prevalent during Grant's administration had led to the formation of a splinter group in the Republican party. These called themselves the Liberal Republicans, and nominated New York *Tribune* editor Horace Greeley for president in 1872. He didn't have a chance against Grant.

It was during Grant's terms in office that the Republican party underwent a metamorphosis, becoming the party supported by and supportive of big business, Western exploiters of the nation's natural resources, and the owners of large farms. Grant's second campaign was financed in large part by millionaires of doubtful background. And wealthy men were greatly admired, in turn, by Grant, who had throughout much of his life found it difficult to earn a decent living.

Vice-President Wilson suffered a stroke just after the election and, though he always denied reports of ill health, this might explain his curiously poor performance as presiding officer of the Senate. Two years later, in November 1875, he suffered a second and fatal stroke.

The United States celebrated its Centennial with a world's fair in Philadelphia. Also in 1876, Custer had his Last Stand in Montana and Alexander Graham Bell exhibited an invention: the telephone. The empty vice-president's chair was hardly noticed.

William Almon Wheeler

A Well-Intentioned Nonentity

REPUBLICAN
IN OFFICE: 1877–1881
PRESIDENT: RUTHERFORD B. HAYES

When president-elect Rutherford B. Hayes asked, "Who is Wheeler?" he asked an unanswerable question. The man who would serve Hayes as vice-president was as close to a nobody as a person can be and still have a physical presence. What we do know about him is that he was honest and had a character of "sterling gold," (according to Hayes, later). When Congress voted itself a raise in pay in the "Salary Grab" of 1873, Wheeler voted against this and returned what he received. We can also assume that he was not a dynamic legislator; from his ten years of service in the House, there is only one piece of legislation that bears his name.

Wheeler's background was one of such poverty that for a time, while he was studying at the University of Vermont, he was forced to live on bread and water for weeks longer than he thought fair. As a result of this

WILLIAM A. WHEELER
(Photographers: Mathew Brady and Levin Handy. Collections of the Library of Congress)

deprivation, he developed a severe case of hypochondria, from which he never recovered.

While still a teenager, Wheeler was elected town clerk of Malone, New York. A Whig early in his career as lawyer and politician, with the dissolution of the Whig party he joined the Republicans and took an interest in civil service reform. Unassuming and unambitious, he married a woman who knew what she wanted and who pushed her husband where she wanted him to be. Unfortunately, she died just before he became vice-president, leaving him in a job he never wanted and dangerously close to a job he wanted even less.

Wheeler's nomination for vice-president may have been the result of a kind of black humor. The convention, in Cincinnati, had nominated an Ohio man for president against the express wishes of New York party boss Roscoe Conkling. New York was given the opportunity to name the number-two man. There appeared to have been a great amount of hilarity on the part of the exuberant but convention-weary delegates as they tossed names back and forth and then finally rushed Wheeler through on the first ballot. Wheeler himself could not have been amused. He had once told a reporter that "any man is foolish to want to be vice-president, unless he cares nothing for active life, and is willing to be a nonentity in the great debates which go on in his presence, without being able to express an opinion."

It must have seemed for a while that Wheeler's wish merely to go home would come true, since in the election the Democratic candidates, Samuel Tilden and Thomas Hendricks, had 300,000 more popular votes than the Republicans and 184 electoral votes to the Republicans' 166. But 185 votes were necessary to win the election, and matters degenerated into a dirty free-for-all involving force and intimidation to gain the necessary votes.

The votes of three Southern states, South Carolina, Florida, and Louisiana, were in doubt and claimed by both parties. The question of these had to be decided by a congressional electoral commission composed of seven Democrats, seven Republicans, and one supposed neutral—who just happened to spend a lot of time chatting with the Republicans on the commission. The Republicans won, eight to seven, and the presidency seemed to have been stolen outright from the Democrats. The Democrats agreed not to make a fuss, however, when a compromise was worked out that promised new roads and railroads and that the last federal troops would be removed from the South. This last effectively ended Reconstruction and helped to assure that the Southern states would be Democratic for years to come.

Hayes was a somewhat unusual president. The three-time governor of Ohio said he would only serve one term in the White House, and he meant it. This may explain how he had the courage to fire Conkling's protégé (and the future vice-president), Chester Alan Arthur, from his lucrative post as collector of the Port of New York as a start toward cleaning up the civil service.

Hayes also had an unusually close personal relationship with his vice-president. Widower Wheeler spent many an evening singing hymns with the president and his wife, "Lemonade Lucy," so called because she refused to have alcoholic beverages in the White House.

In his diary, Hayes described Wheeler as "one of the few Vice-Presidents who were on cordial terms—intimate and friendly with the President." Nevertheless, Wheeler was bored and unhappy as vice-president and was as pleased as he was capable of being when it was over. When a newspaperman wrote of his death six years later that "it was hard to mark the exact moment of its [Wheeler's life's] flight," he may have meant that it made so little difference it might have happened years before.

Chester Alan Arthur

The Quintessential Party Hack

REPUBLICAN
IN OFFICE: 1881
PRESIDENT: JAMES GARFIELD

The only political office that Chester Arthur was ever elected to was the vice-presidency, from which he went on to inhabit the White House. The thought of succeeding to the presidency had probably never occurred to him—or to anyone else. But when Arthur became the third vice-president to be promoted to the highest office in the land, the possible demise of even healthy young presidents could no longer be considered unlikely.

James Garfield did not win the presidential nomination at the Republican convention of 1880 until the thirty-sixth ballot, when the main contenders had exhausted themselves fighting. New Yorker Levi Parsons Morton was the convention's first choice for vice-president, but he turned it down, thinking it unlikely that Garfield could win. Eight years later, he would not make the same mistake.

CHESTER A. ARTHUR

(Artist: Ole Peter Hansen Balling. National Portrait Gallery, Smithsonian Institution, Washington, D.C.)

Arthur's subsequent nomination was supposed to placate New York senator Roscoe Conkling, who had tried but failed to win sufficient support for Grant for an unprecedented third term. At this time, Conkling was one of the two most powerful "bosses" in American politics. The other was Maine senator James G. Blaine, his political enemy. Their followers were known, respectively, as the Stalwarts and the Half-Breeds. (The Half-Breeds' name referred to their mongrel-like mixture of liberals and independents who favored civil service reform. The Stalwarts were the conservatives of the party who opposed reform, and stalwart remains a term for a loyal party worker.) Arthur had been a disciple and crony of Conkling for thirteen years. Though often caricatured as a political hack, Arthur was a dignified man who dressed with sartorial elegance, displayed real abilities as an attorney, and understood perfectly the secrets of running a political machine.

Patronage was then a politician's principal source of power, and Conkling controlled thousands of civil service jobs. He had appointed Arthur to the top position at the New York Customs House, an extremely lucrative job that in turn controlled some 2,500 additional appointments. Conkling and Arthur were understandably livid when President Hayes, under pressure from civil service reformers within the Republican party, forced Arthur to resign.

To prevent the reform business from getting out of hand, Conkling wanted to bring Grant back as the Republican presidential nominee; Grant's fondness for the patronage system was well known. But the 1880 convention was a stubborn, wayward creature, and even

"Lord Roscoe" could not control it. Upset at not being able to resurrect Grant, Conkling left the convention floor before the voting was over and missed Arthur's nomination for the vice-presidency.

Arthur later found Conkling sulking in a press room, where a scene reminiscent of one between parent and adolescent then took place. While Arthur pleaded for understanding, Conkling scolded.

Arthur: "The Ohio men have offered me the Vice-presidency."

Conkling: "Well son, you should drop it as you would a red-hot shoe from the forge."

Arthur: "I thought to consult, not . . ."

Conkling: "What is there to consult about? This trickster of Mentor [Garfield] will be defeated before the country."

Arthur: "There is something else to be said. The office of Vice-president is a greater honor than I ever dreamed of attaining. A barren nomination would be a great honor. In a calmer moment you will look at this differently."

Conkling: "If you wish for my respect you will contemptuously decline it."

Arthur: "Senator Conkling, I shall accept the nomination and shall carry the majority of the delegation."

Conkling was too enraged to say more, but did, in a calmer moment, come to terms with the nomination. Others found it hard to stomach the honor's going to a party hack who had never been elected to anything. Former Secretary of the Treasury John Sherman, in what may have been a fit of pique at just missing the presidential nod himself, considered Arthur's selection as "rather a scandalous procedure," and claimed his nomination was "a ridiculous burlesque and . . . inspired by a desire to beat the ticket." In an editorial in the *Nation*, Edwin Lawrence Godkin favored Arthur's nomination, but only because it would remove him from the New York scene and tie him to an office where "his powers of mischief" would be small. In the same piece, Godkin made mention of the prospect of Garfield's death, which may have prescient on the editor's part but was unfortunately inaccurate: he considered the possibility "too unlikely a contingency to be worth making [any] extraordinary provision for."

Garfield defeated the Democratic nominee General Winfield S. Hancock of Pennsylvania, but his presidency lasted less than two hundred days after the inauguration. While walking through Washington's Pennsylvania Station with Secretary of State Blaine, on his way to address his alma mater, Williams College, he was shot twice by Charles Guiteau. Guiteau was severely disgruntled—almost incoherent—at not getting one of the 100,000 federal jobs available; during his trial he exhibited obvious reasons for an insanity plea but was hanged regardless. Garfield did not die, however, for almost three months and might have survived, it is speculated, if the instruments used in his treatment had been properly sterilized.

As he fired, Guiteau had cried, "I am a Stalwart and Arthur is President now!"—which did not make the transition any easier for Arthur. Even one of his friends was heard to exclaim, "Chet Arthur, President of the United States! Good God!" And yet, Arthur managed to rise to the occasion. He especially confounded critics who had expected him to be dominated by Conkling. As

Arthur once declared, "For the Vice-presidency, I was indebted to Mr. Conkling, but for the Presidency of the United States my debt is to the Almighty." And this onetime master of the patronage system even signed the Pendleton Civil Service Act into law, requiring examinations of those seeking federal positions.

Chester Arthur had no vice-president. And he took very good care of himself.

Thomas Andrews Hendricks

"The Professional Candidate"

DEMOCRAT

IN OFFICE: 1885

PRESIDENT: GROVER CLEVELAND

"Give it to him for God's sake" was the rally cry of Hendricks's nomination in 1884 for Democratic vice-president. Not exactly a ringing endorsement, but that was the way people felt about this persistent contender for high office. He was called by some "The Professional Candidate." Hendricks and onetime presidential candidate Samuel J. Tilden had come within a corrupt vote of winning the election eight years earlier, and his name had been put in nomination for either the presidency or the vice-presidency three other times. When the aging, sickly Tilden was told that Hendricks would like to be on the ticket with him again, he knowingly responded, "I do not wonder, considering my weakness."

Hendricks was a typical party man, enjoying the spoils system and working his way up the political ladder from the Indiana Senate to the U.S. House of Representatives and, later, to the U.S. Senate (1863–1869) and then either over or down to a term as Indiana's governor. He did not seem to place much store by this iast office, saying he felt that "any man competent to be a notary public could be Governor of Indiana." And he did not leave much of an imprint in any office; his lack of strong beliefs led Indiana senator Oliver P. Morton to refer to him as "The Artful Dodger." Morton also said that Hendricks's thirty years of nonachievement in office set some sort of record.

The Boston *Journal* expressed the view of the Republicans and of many in Hendricks's own party when it declared that he was "an amiable politician of the shilly-shallying order on the financial and other leading questions." A contemporary summed him up by saying that "he might have been a statesman if he had been less of a demagogue . . . Instead of leading his people, he was ready to yield to any clamor and foster any delusion that promised him votes."

On one subject, however, Hendricks's views were well known. He came out strongly against the Emancipation Proclamation, the Thirteenth Amendment to abolish slavery, and the Fourteenth Amendment guaranteeing citizenship rights to blacks, because, he said, the Negro was "inferior and no good would come from his freedom." This may sound shocking in a candidate for national office, but a hundred years ago it earned the backing of the South and of Hendricks's own state, Indiana.

Geography played a larger part than usual in the convention of 1884, because winning the states of New York and Indiana could mean the difference between win-

THOMAS A. HENDRICKS
(Artist: George E. Perine. National Portrait Gallery, Smithsonian Institution, Washington, D.C.)

ning and losing the election. And the Democrats were tired of losing. New York's very large governor, three-hundred pound Grover Cleveland, and Indiana's medium-sized politician-of-many-offices were both placed in nomination for the presidency, but Hendricks's friends could never muster more than 45½ votes for their man, depressingly short of the 547 necessary. And once his little bandwagon had stalled, Hendricks was tossed the vice-presidential bone.

The campaign was an especially dirty one, there being plenty of ammunition on both sides for mudslinging. The Republican candidate, Blaine of Maine, had the incriminating "Mulligan" letters, which showed him guilty of selling his influence, to explain. And Cleveland had to rise above the scandal of his affair, more than ten years previously, with the Widow Halpin and its resulting illegitimate offspring, for whom he assumed responsibility. His honesty ("Whatever you do, tell the truth") won him forgiveness by most, although he might not have been so lucky if women had had the vote.

Cleveland did not have much support from his running mate: Hendricks went around telling people that he thought Cleveland should withdraw because of the paternity issue, and he never quite gave up the idea that he should have been the presidential candidate. The New York *Nation* reacted to one of his speeches by writing: "We must take the liberty of warning the Democrats that Mr. Hendricks, already a heavy load to carry, may readily become heavier by making speeches. He is in some respects a ridiculous nomination and would be worse than ridiculous if he were to have any political duties."

The Republican party, split by a group of intellectuals called Mugwumps, who were pro-reform and anti-Blaine, lost the presidency for the first time in twenty-four years.

The vice-presidency never gave Hendricks much satisfaction, because Cleveland did not play by the rules of the patronage system, as Hendricks knew and loved them. He once groused that "the Democratic party isn't in power. Grover Cleveland is making a party of his own." Hendricks was quite right in telling a friend that he would "never be a candidate for . . . any office again." He knew that, because of two strokes suffered before the convention, he would probably not live out his term. Most people knew that the sixty-five-year-old man was sickly and doddering but, since he was keeping the extent of his poor health a secret, everyone but his wife was surprised when he died nine months after taking office—once they realized he was gone.

Levi Parsons Morton

The Model Presiding Officer

REPUBLICAN
IN OFFICE: 1889–1893
PRESIDENT: BENJAMIN HARRISON

The Republican convention of 1880 had offered Levi Parsons Morton the vice-presidential position on the ticket with James Garfield, but New York party boss Roscoe Conkling, in one of his fits of pique, told him to refuse it. Morton's thoughts can only be imagined when fellow New York machine man Chester Alan Arthur rebelled against Conkling, took the nomination, and then went on to succeed to the presidency.

Eight years later, the New York delegates again had the choice of vice-president, because the man they had supported for president, Blaine of Maine, was defeated at the convention by Benjamin Harrison of Indiana. Morton, then sixty-four years old, was again offered the job, and this time no one was going to talk him out of it.

Morton was probably the nation's richest vice-presi-

LEVI P. MORTON
(Artist: Léon-Joseph Florentin Bonnat. National Portrait Gallery, Smithsonian Institution, Washington, D.C.)

dent up to that time, but his political background was skimpy. He had twice run unsuccessfully for the Senate and the only elective office he had ever held was that of congressman for two years. He had hoped to be President Garfield's secretary of the treasury but was instead named ambassador to France, where he served for four years. Entertaining European royalty was not, however, a training course for executive power in the U.S. government.

But Morton's nomination in 1888 was not as madcap as it might appear. His great wealth was not inherited, so he obviously had the ability to rise above a poor childhood and the lack of college education. He made a fortune as a dry goods merchant and then made even more by going into international banking. This gave him access not only to funds but to other wealthy people, and he was an expert campaign fund raiser for the Thomas Platt–Roscoe Conkling Republican machine in New York City. The Republicans were well pleased with their man when he managed not only to increase the party coffers but to win his state for the party over fellow New Yorker, Grover Cleveland, who was up for presidential reelection on the Democratic ticket.

In many respects, Morton was the perfect vice-president. He enjoyed meeting visiting dignitaries and royalty and could afford to entertain them with lavish parties, a chore that fell more and more often to vice-presidents with their apparently idle hours. Edwin G. Lowry described this job in the Washington periodical, *Close-Ups*, writing: "His dress clothes are his working clothes, the overalls of a Vice President . . . Every night from November until May he must sally forth in his glad raiment, and eat for his party and his chief."

Morton took presiding over the Senate very seriously. He was "the model presiding officer," so scrupulously fair in dealing with disputes that his own party several times suggested that he take a vacation so that they could settle things to their liking. On one occasion, Morton would not even leave the chamber for lunch, because he knew the Republicans planned to rush votes through behind his back.

This sense of fairness led to both parties' giving Morton a farewell banquet of appreciation when his term was up. Nebraska senator Charles Manderson toasted him, saying, "In the history of the country this is the first instance where the Vice-President about to retire to private life has been thus complimented by those who have been his associates in the Senate . . ." Manderson went on to mention that Morton had been forced to listen to "something more than 475 morning prayers, and to the unpremeditated art of seventy or more senatorial eulogies" without being able to hide in the cloakroom; he could do nothing but "sit and take it."

Morton's evenhandedness in the Senate disinclined his party to renominate him for a second term with Harrison. For Morton's sake it is nice to know that Harrison lost anyway. Political wags answered the question of why Morton was not renominated by saying: "God was good to him."

The year after leaving national office, Morton was elected governor of New York—at considerable personal expense—but after one term decided to leave the political life and retire to his one-thousand-acre farm in Rhinebeck, New York. His retirement lasted a very long time: he lived to be ninety-six years old.

Adlai Ewing Stevenson

"The Axeman"

DEMOCRAT
IN OFFICE: 1893–1897
PRESIDENT: GROVER CLEVELAND

The election of 1892 was unique in that it returned to office a president who had been defeated for reelection four years earlier. Grover Cleveland was able to bring this off partly because the recently widowed Republican candidate, Benjamin Harrison, did not have much zeal for campaigning. For the first time, too, there was—at least vocally—a strong third party, the People's party, or Populists, whose cry was for silver coinage, a graduated income tax, paper currency, and other ideas radical at that time. They received 22 electoral votes out of a total of 144.

On Cleveland's instructions, Adlai Stevenson of Illinois was nominated for Democratic vice-president, because of his views on silver inflation. He was considered a "soft money" man, who might draw some Populist votes in spite of Cleveland's opposing views.

ADLAI E. STEVENSON
(Collections of the Library of Congress)

Stevenson also appealed to Democratic party regulars; they remembered with relish the enthusiasm he had displayed in dispensing patronage during Cleveland's first administration. As first assistant postmaster general, he had known just what to do after twenty-four years of Republicans in the White House: 40,000 Republican postmasters were replaced by 40,000 Democratic postmasters with such alacrity that Stevenson became known as the "Axeman," or "Headsman." He once claimed that "the highest compliment he had ever received" was that he had "decapitated sixty-five Republican postmasters in two minutes." This healthy respect for the spoils system on the part of the 1892 vice-presidential nominee gladdened the hearts of the Democratic "boys" who remembered Cleveland's reluctance during his 1885–1889 term to participate in patronage—his "treacherous conduct toward the party he claims to represent," as one disgusted senator put it. Party reformers could rationalize, on the other hand, that as vice-president the Axeman would not be in a position to dispense patronage.

Stevenson was an attractive candidate—charming, witty, a great raconteur, and possessed of a certain "magnetism" that made him popular with the crowds. A contemporary described him as a country lawyer who "practiced politics about as much as he practiced his profession; his profession, for profit, politics, for sheer joy. He was one of the most popular campaigners in the land, and . . . the delight of the multitude." His appeal can be seen in the fact that he handily won election in the Republican stronghold of Illinois; the state sent Stevenson, a Democrat, to Congress twice and broke a thirty-two-year Republican voting record by going with the Democrats when Stevenson ran with Cleveland.

Affable though Stevenson was, the party leadership was not anxious for the monetary liberal's career to progress any further. They were horrified when doctors found a malignant growth on the roof of Cleveland's mouth in 1893. To avoid false or undue fears, arrangements were made to keep the president's condition secret. An operation to remove part of his jaw and palate was performed on a friend's yacht as it slowly cruised up the East River in New York. Cleveland was soon back at work, dental work being used as the cover story for the padding around the new fake jawbone in his mouth. The true story was not admitted to the public until 1917, nine years after Cleveland's demise, so it must have been something else that caused a Stevenson critic to remark, "There goes the Vice President with nothing on his mind but the state of the President's health." This seems to be a harsh assessment, although the two executives were never close because of their too different approaches to politics.

Stevenson served in the middle of what were termed the Gay Nineties, but what was really more a time of considerable trouble. There was a depression, and more than 2,000,000 workers were unemployed. The conflict between the haves and the have-nots culminated in labor disturbances such as the Pullman strike, led by Eugene Debs, and the march to the Capitol of Coxey's army of unemployed protestors.

In 1900, Stevenson was again nominated to run for vice-president, this time with William Jennings Bryan.

The silver Republicans and one wing of the Populists also nominated him, but none of them could return him to office. That left him free to spend time with his grandson and namesake, whom he advised never to seek the vice-presidency. The boy, Adlai Ewing Stevenson II, took his advice and ran (unsuccessfully) for president, in 1952 and 1956, instead.

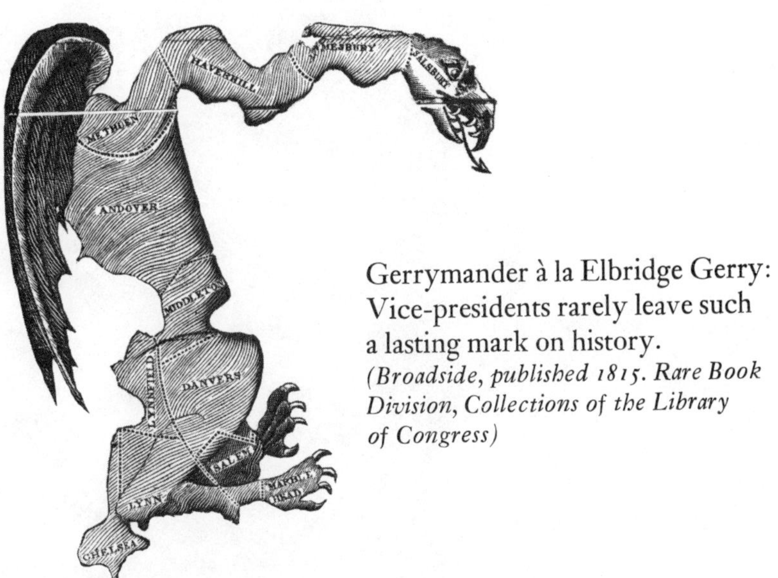

Gerrymander à la Elbridge Gerry: Vice-presidents rarely leave such a lasting mark on history.
(Broadside, published 1815. Rare Book Division, Collections of the Library of Congress)

Aaron Burr/Alexander Hamilton duel: Murder by a vice-president is rare—but it happens.
(19th-century print, photographed by Bain News Service. Collections of the Library of Congress)

Abraham Lincoln/Hannibal Hamlin: Campaign posters have changed little in substance.
(Currier & Ives. National Portrait Gallery, Smithsonian Institution, Washington, D. C.)

William McKinley and Garret Hobart: Vice-presidents seldom find themselves this close to the president.
(Pach Bros. Studio. National Portrait Gallery, Smithsonian Institution, Washington, D. C.)

Teddy Roosevelt and Rough Riders: Vice-presidents often have their own set of admirers.
(Photo by Allen Davison. Collections of the Library of Congress)

Calvin Coolidge: The number-two man often performs duties for which the chief executive has no time.
(Bain News Service. Collections of the Library of Congress)

John Nance Garner in 1955: Retired vice-presidents go on to various activities.
(UPI photo. Collections of the Library of Congress)

Richard M. Nixon: Vice-presidents are often called on to entertain and be entertained.
(AP photo. Collections of the Library of Congress)

Garret Augustus Hobart

"Assistant President"

REPUBLICAN
IN OFFICE: 1897–1899
PRESIDENT: WILLIAM MCKINLEY

Although little remembered today, Garret Hobart possessed several of the qualities of an ideal vice-president. He was in agreement with the president on all the important issues, or at least discreet enough so that no one would know there were differences. His home state of New Jersey set enough of a geographical "balance" to avoid offending more than half the nation. He had enough wealth (honestly earned) so that visiting royalty and dignitaries could be entertained in such style that it would not be embarrassing to the American people. And politics was not a passion, just an interesting hobby for a person who had made all the money he could ever need and had served on too many committees. Our lack of knowledge of Vice-President Hobart is due in part to the fact that his death was somewhat premature—only two years into the administration.

GARRET A. HOBART
(Collections of the Library of Congress)

He had accumulated a bit of a fortune in his law practice in New Jersey and as director of several corporations and president of some banks and a couple of railroads and of the Passaic Water Company. His financial acumen would endear him to President William McKinley, who, because he was so often in debt himself, stood in awe of those who knew how to handle money. Hobart was in agreement with the presidential nominee and most other Republicans on the big issue of the day —the support of the gold standard—and in opposition to Democratic candidate William Jennings Bryan, who would give his "Cross of Gold" speech to enthusiastic crowds across the country.

For a man who found public speaking painful, Hobart did manage to say one memorable, though not entirely accurate, thing in his nomination acceptance speech. He claimed that an "honest dollar, worth one hundred cents, cannot be carved out of fifty-three cents worth of silver plus a government fiat." After that he went home and quietly made certain that normally Democratic New Jersey voted Republican.

McKinley, who apparently did not feel the need to overexpose himself to the public, or vice versa, conducted a "front porch campaign" from his home in Canton, Ohio, giving speeches to the trainloads of people who made the pilgrimage there. And he still defeated the peripatetic Bryan. This lesson on underexposure has obviously gone unheeded in American political life since that time. The campaign of the two Republican strong, silent types was in the hands of Mark Hanna, a wealthy Ohio businessman who so admired McKinley that he managed the election almost single-handedly. He raised millions in campaign funds from bankers and businessmen by appealing to their fears of the "radical" Bryan.

The Chicago *News* wrote of the election of Hobart that "he will not be seen or heard from until after four years when he emerges from the impenetrable vacuum called the Vice-Presidency." This was quickly proven wrong. Although Hobart's political experience had been limited to being state senator and chairman of the New Jersey Republican Committee, he managed to earn the vice-presidency a considerable amount of respect and prestige. In fact, he insisted on it. Columbia University professor Nicholas Butler said that Hobart was the "best presiding officer . . . the Senate has ever had in my lifetime." Henry Cabot Lodge felt that Hobart had "restored the vice-presidency to its proper position." Some went so far as to call Hobart the "Assistant President" because of the effectiveness of his liaison with the Senate and the strength of his position as adviser to the president. Historian Louis Hatch claimed that Hobart's influence was "probably greater than any other vice-president has enjoyed."

Being wealthy allowed Hobart and his wife to throw some great parties in the evenings in their rented mansion across from the White House. In the afternoon, Mrs. Hobart would open the windows and leave the room while her husband entertained congressmen at his "smokers." When McKinley joined the festivities, he and Hobart worked together to persuade the legislators of the value of their programs.

War fever was rising at this time, due in large part to the hysteria of the "yellow press," which was calling for Cuban independence from Spain. McKinley and his party resisted as long as they could in the hope of avoiding anything that would put a crimp in their booming business concerns. After the sinking of the battleship *Maine* in Havana harbor in 1898, they could no longer keep the peace honorably. Hobart was asked to sit in on cabinet meetings during the ensuing Spanish-American War, which was mercifully brief (ten weeks) and immensely successful for the United States.

Because of his closeness to the president, Hobart was privy to McKinley's divinely inspired answer to "the Philippine problem." The problem was what to do with the Philippine Islands, which had been liberated from the Spanish along with Cuba. McKinley's decision, as revealed to him during prayer, was "to educate the Filipinos, and uplift and civilize and Christianize them . . . and to put the Philippines on the map of the United States." That settled, Hobart broke the tie in the Senate by voting against Philippine independence. The result was three years of war in a country reluctant to accept McKinley's plans for it.

It is not known whether it was high living, too many cigars, or too much unaccustomed authority that weakened his cardiovascular system, but when Hobart was only fifty-five years old he went home to New Jersey for a visit and died of heart failure.

Theodore Roosevelt

"That Damned Cowboy"

REPUBLICAN
IN OFFICE: 1901
PRESIDENT: WILLIAM MCKINLEY

There have been other ambitious vice-presidents: Burr, Calhoun, Nixon. And intelligent vice-presidents: Jefferson, Wallace. And charismatic vice-presidents: Stevenson, Breckinridge. There have been patriotic vice-presidents: John Adams, Andrew Johnson. And verbose vice-presidents: Humphrey, Dawes. There have been others who were lucky, who had large families, and who had wealthy, privileged backgrounds. But there had never been a vice-president who embodied all these qualities until Theodore Roosevelt. It is interesting to speculate on what he might have done to or for the office if he had been in it for a full term. Or would the office have defeated even him?

There is no denying that Roosevelt had dreamed of being in the White House, but he did not consider the vice-presidency the route to get there. It was "not a stepping stone to anything but oblivion," he said. He did not even think he had "sufficient means" to be vice-president and said he would not mind if he were in the Senate or the cabinet but that he would "want to consider . . . when the office is in fact merely a show office." Active jobs such as secretary of war or the governor generalship of the Philippines were what he would intend to push for in McKinley's second administration. Events and political bosses had other plans for him. His friends—notably Massachusetts senator Henry Cabot Lodge—wanted to advance his career; his enemies—notably New York senator Thomas Platt—wanted to bring it to an end. Cabot and Platt both felt that the vice-presidency was the answer.

At the time of all this maneuvering, Roosevelt was governor of New York, a natural power base from which to run for president in 1904. But Senator Platt, who controlled the state's Republican party, now regretted giving his blessings to Teddy's election and wanted him out of office. Not that there was anything Platt could have done to stop Roosevelt's becoming governor (1899–1900). Teddy had come back as a national hero from the charge up San Juan Hill in the "bully war"—his words —in Cuba. His Rough Riders adored him, and the country adored them all. One army regular, in speaking of their popularity, observed: "There were possibly 1,100 men in the Rough Riders, and I have personally known 15,000 of them."

Before quitting civilian life to join the army, Roosevelt had been assistant secretary of the navy and one of the strongest advocates of war with the Spanish. It was

THEODORE ROOSEVELT
(Artist: Adrian Lamb. National Portrait Gallery, Smithsonian Institution, Washington, D.C.)

while McKinley was vacillating and hoping to avoid a disruption of prosperous good times that Roosevelt compared the president's backbone to a chocolate éclair. He also took it upon himself, when his boss was out of town, to notify the navy to be on the alert ("Keep full of coal"), with the result that the U.S. Navy under Admiral George Dewey was able to destroy the Spanish fleet in the waters of the Philippines.

Before all this, Roosevelt had been police commissioner of New York City, a job he did with considerable élan but little real effectiveness. Before that he had been appointed to the U.S. Civil Service Commission under President Harrison, where he performed with more noise and effect than most politicians were comfortable with. And before that had come his auspicious political beginnings in the New York State legislature.

Even before all this, Roosevelt conquered an asthmatic, sickly childhood; he endured the loss of his first wife and his mother, both of whom died on the same day; he bought and worked a cattle ranch in the Dakotas; he became an avid naturalist and hunter; and he wrote several histories and biographies. It took a healthy ego as well as incredible energy to accomplish all these things. Speaker of the House Tom Reed once tried to bring Teddy down a peg by saying, "Theodore, if there is one thing more than another for which I admire you, it is for your original discovery of the Ten Commandments!"

In 1900, the vice-presidential question loomed. Roosevelt was flattered, but wary. He had once claimed that he would rather be a professor of history than vice-president, and rushed to Washington to assure the Mc-

Kinley administration that he did not seek the position. Secretary of War Elihu Root did not really put Roosevelt's mind at rest by saying, "Of course not, Theodore, you're not fit for it." "Kingmaker" Mark Hanna, appalled at the fact that there would be "only one life between this madman and the White House," urged McKinley to come out for someone else, but the president saw that the tide for Teddy was too strong to be stopped, and wisely remained neutral. Roosevelt's arrival at the convention in his Rough Rider hat brought the delegates to their feet in enthusiasm. He modestly said that if they really wanted him, he could not "seem to be bigger than the party"; he won the nomination for vice-president.

Journalist William Allen White saw Roosevelt's nomination as an effort "not to praise him but to bury him," and Platt gloated that he was going down to Washington "to see Theodore Roosevelt take the veil." Teddy began to feel the same way, complaining, "I fear my bolt is shot," and was sure he would now have time to complete his law studies.

As vice-president, he only had to preside in the Senate—a task for which he had no proclivity or ability—for five days before there was a recess; New York senator Chauncey Depew judged his performance there as lacking "the impartiality, equitable temper and knowledge of parliamentary law to be a good presiding officer." President McKinley soon ignored him, and the vice-president felt that "he does not intend that I shall have any influence of any kind . . . This he has made evident again and again." So Roosevelt went on a speaking tour to show the crowds what he felt they might expect in the White House four years later.

It turned out to be *less than a year later*, because anarchist Leon Czolgosz "thought it would be a good thing for the country to kill the President," and did so when the president was visiting Buffalo, New York, September 6, 1901. McKinley died a week later. Mark Hanna expressed the feelings of many people when he said, "Now look, that damned cowboy is President of the U.S." But "that damned cowboy" would become the first "accidental" president to win renomination and reelection, and may have made the vice-presidency alluring enough to tempt ambitious men like F.D.R. and J.F.K. to later try for it.

Commenting on his incredible energy, the Boston Sunday *Globe* once said of Theodore Roosevelt: "It would never do . . . to permit such a man to get into the Presidency. He would produce national insomnia." And Teddy was a dynamic leader. A British ambassador explained Roosevelt's ebullience with the remark, "You must always remember that the President is about six."

Charles Warren Fairbanks

Back to Basics

REPUBLICAN
IN OFFICE: 1905–1909
PRESIDENT: THEODORE ROOSEVELT

The Republican party returned to business as usual in its next two vice-presidential nominees. For Charles Fairbanks and James Sherman, while not exactly nonentities, were lackluster choices compared to Roosevelt. (The Democratic vice-presidential candidate, running with New York judge Alton B. Parker, was eighty-year-old millionaire Henry Gassaway, one of the oldest ever nominated.)

Alaskans may have known something about Fairbanks that was not apparent to the mainland states, because they named their second-largest city for him (as senator, he chaired the joint commission to settle Alaskan disputes). Geographically, Indianan Fairbanks was a good "balance" for New Yorker Roosevelt; politically, he was too conservative for the president. He also had the now-dubious distinction of being a "born in a log cabin"

CHARLES W. FAIRBANKS
(Collections of the Library of Congress)

politician. His political rise came from the usual combination of ambition, money, and party hackwork. Eventually he came to believe that this combustible mixture had earned him and qualified him for the presidency, with the vice-presidency merely a step along the way.

Fairbanks made his considerable fortune by acting as attorney for bankrupt railroads and then becoming their chief officer or president. As a wealthy man, he had a loud voice in his state's Republican party politics, and in 1896 he was the keynote speaker at the national convention that nominated William McKinley for president. A year later, Fairbanks was elected to the U.S. Senate. McKinley's campaign manager, Mark Hanna, suggested Fairbanks for the vice-presidential spot in McKinley's second term but, according to journalist and author Henry Luther Stoddard, "Fairbanks had dreams of the White House. He preferred to remain in the Senate until the real call came." Like Levi Morton, Fairbanks must have cursed his lack of foresight when Roosevelt succeeded thanks to the president's assassination.

Roosevelt would not have chosen an old-guard politician like Fairbanks for his running mate in 1904, but even presidential nominees have only so much leverage. Teddy had used his up in obtaining the chairmanship of the Republican National Committee for his personal friend George B. Cortelyou, America's first secretary of commerce and labor.

Roosevelt had once advocated that the president consult with the vice-president regularly on all important issues and even give him a seat in the cabinet. But to the president, Fairbanks remained just another "reactionary machine politician" whom he completely ignored. The story goes that, when a chandelier's tinkling in the White House was disturbing Teddy's sleep, he ordered the butler to remove it. When the butler asked where he should take it, Roosevelt replied, "Take it to the Vice President, he needs something to keep him awake."

As vice-president, Fairbanks made an effort to maintain a power base but found that without the ability to give patronage he had no constructive role to play. With reactionary House Speaker "Uncle Joe" Cannon, he attempted to thwart Roosevelt's Square Deal reform program and promised to bury "all progressive measures in committee so that they [will] never come to vote." And he did not hesitate to rule speakers out of order if they stepped over the bounds of his political priorities. He claimed to be "on the alert to rule any dangerous speakers 'out of order' on the slightest pretext."

Fairbanks's ambitions for the presidency never died and were so blatant that Chicago humorist Finley Peter Dunne once advised Roosevelt not to take a planned submarine trip—"unless you take Fairbanks with you." Roosevelt, who was working to have his secretary of war, Robert Taft, succeed him in the presidency in 1909, discussed Fairbanks's ambitions for the position in a letter to a friend: "Do you know who we have the most trouble in beating! . . . Fairbanks! Think of it—Charley Fairbanks! I was never more surprised in my life . . . He's got a hold in Kentucky, Indiana and some other states that is hard to break. How and why is beyond me."

Taft won the nomination and election, and four years later Fairbanks acted in vengeance by working to defeat Roosevelt and his Bull Moose party. In 1916, Fairbanks was again his party's vice-presidential candidate on the ticket with Charles Evans Hughes, but they lost a very close contest to the team of Woodrow Wilson and Thomas Marshall. Exhausted by all his election misses and near-misses, Fairbanks died in 1918.

James Schoolcraft Sherman

"Dollar Jim"

REPUBLICAN
IN OFFICE: 1909–1912
PRESIDENT: WILLIAM HOWARD TAFT

There is something to be said for "balancing" a ticket politically: it helps to unite different factions of the party and keeps it from splintering off into small interest groups. But if the principle is carried to extremes, it can jeopardize the intent of the administration. Such was the case with Roosevelt and Fairbanks and with Taft and Sherman.

"Sunny Jim" Sherman was a lawyer and wealthy businessman form Utica, New York, who had inherited the New Hartford Canning Company and became president of the Utica Trust Company. Rejecting his family's Democratic affiliations, he was elected Utica's Republican mayor when he was just twenty-nine, and went on later to serve as U.S. congressman for twenty years. There is no major legislation bearing his name, but he became a close friend and political ally of Speakers

JAMES S. SHERMAN
(Collections of the Library of Congress)

Thomas Reed and then Joseph Cannon, serving several times as Speaker pro tem himself.

In 1906, Sherman was chairman of the New York Republican convention and introduced a plan to have all Republicans donate a dollar to the campaign. This earned him a second nickname: "Dollar Jim." Two years later, when the conservative Republicans were casting about for a running mate for President Roosevelt's handpicked presidential candidate, Ohioan William Howard Taft, they found one of their own in Sunny Jim. (The Democrats decided to go with Bryan for the third time.)

For Sherman, the nomination was "an honor which I wanted but had little thought of securing," but for others, such as the editors of the *Nation*, it was "proof of the flippant way in which Americans . . . fill . . . the highest offices."

The Republicans were a heavyweight team; Sherman and Taft together would have tipped the scales at more than 500 pounds. There were some, however, who considered Sherman's looks a drawback, because with his "perceptible though not aggressive" side whiskers he looked too English to appeal to the large Irish vote. The New York *Tribune* described him as weighing in "at about 225 pounds, and [he] looks as jolly as his somewhat heavier running-mate Mr. Taft. Generally he wears a square-topped derby hat, an English walking coat, maybe a green or purple waistcoat and conspicuous spectacles. His face is round and his smile is rarely missing."

At the beginning of their four years together, Taft and Sherman got along fairly well and socialized over games of golf. This continued until Taft discovered not only that his vice-president would not go along with his reform programs but that he did not play golf very well. On the second matter, Taft was tenderhearted and felt "committed to the Vice-President for golf and fears to hurt his feelings by not asking him to join him when he plays."

Their political differences were not so easily overlooked. Taft, who wanted nothing to do with the crusty old ultraconservative, Joseph Cannon, asked Sherman to act as his liaison in the House, but not-so-Sunny Jim showed his true colors and loyalties by replying, "I am vice-president, and acting as a messenger boy is not part of my duties . . ." This sort of thing led Taft to the unoriginal observation that "as a rule the President and the Vice-President seem to drift apart no matter how close they are together at the start." Once, after listening to a Sherman oration sprinkled with biblical quotations, Teddy Roosevelt turned to Taft and remarked, "When Jim Sherman quotes scripture the devil must shake all hell with his laughter." Another time, when the president was quite ill and the stock market fell, he remarked to a friend, "That is strange. I should think when Wall Street thinks of Jim Sherman and his intimates, stocks would go up." When Taft recovered from his malady, he vowed to live "to preserve the country from the sage of Utica."

Meanwhile, back in New York State, a still young Theodore Roosevelt was growing restless in his role as ex-president, and began grumbling about the slowness with which he thought Taft was carrying out his programs. When the state convention was electing its temporary chairman, Roosevelt saw his chance to reenter the political scene, but first he had to eliminate the machine-backed candidate, Sunny Jim. They both sought the backing of Taft, who, not wanting to hurt anyone's feelings, ended up turning both men against him. Roosevelt managed to win the post, but the victory was hollow since the Republicans lost the governorship anyway.

In 1912, Roosevelt decided to come back through the front door and run for the third term as president that he had vowed not to seek four years earlier. When the Republicans rejected him in favor of another term for Taft and Sherman, Teddy stalked out of the convention with his delegates and formed the Bull Moose party. Splitting the Republican party led to the usual outcome: a win for the other party, headed by Woodrow Wilson and Thomas Marshall.

James Sherman did not live to be disappointed. He died less than a week before the election, which led to a curious voting problem. Sherman's name remained on the ballot, and he collected more than three million popular votes. But the eight electoral votes could not be listed for a dead man, so the Republicans gave them to Columbia University professor Nicholas Murray Butler, who agreed to accept them provided, he said, "There was no chance of electing a Republican Vice-President."

Thomas Riley Marshall

An Impish Wit from Indiana

DEMOCRAT

IN OFFICE: 1913–1921

PRESIDENT: WOODROW WILSON

Thomas Marshall, who had served as Indiana governor for four years before his vice-presidency, is probably remembered by most people today for his quip that "What this country needs is a really good five-cent cigar." Years of repetition may have dimmed some of its charm, but the man who coined the phrase was doubtless our wittiest vice-president. The problem with humor in high places is that few people take the man seriously. Wilson, for instance, did not find it amusing when Marshall inscribed a book to him, "From your only vice," and initially wrote his running mate off as a man of "small caliber" intelligence.

Marshall's quick and apparently thoughtless comments made others suspect his political acumen also. When, during World War I, Marshall heard about the sinking of the *Lusitania*, he remarked that anyone on an English

THOMAS R. MARSHALL
(Collections of the Library of Congress)

ship was as good as on English soil and must take the consequences. The *New York Times*, in bombastic fury, replied, "If Indiana cannot raise men of Presidential calibre, she should at least try to train mediocre men in some of the negative virtues . . . to keep silent when they have not the mental equipment to fit them for an understanding of what is required." During the course of war, the *Times* appeared to gain an appreciation of Marshall's outspokenness and said that "the words he speaks have a sense and sanity that are urgently needed." In response to a later verbal sally, the paper showed itself quite smitten, and wrote, "Tom Marshall of Indiana can still be counted on to say the blunt and do the honest thing."

On taking office, Marshall vowed to "acknowledge the insignificant influence of the office; to take it in a good-natured way; to be . . . loyal to my chief and at the same time not to be offensive to my associates." He had refused at first to attend cabinet meetings, saying he would not do the president's work without the president's salary, but became the first vice-president to preside in cabinet meetings when Wilson traveled to Paris to push his peace plan. Much of his time was spent trying to find jobs for his friends, and his office was easily accessible—so much so that he claimed it was not much different from "a monkey cage, except the visitors do not offer me any peanuts." He once remarked that "those who know nothing are placed in the seats of the mighty. The wise men remain at home and discuss public questions on the ends of street cars and around barber shops." This endeared him to streetcar riders and barbers but not to politicians, especially Democratic senators, who considered his leadership of the Senate too impartial.

When the vice-president needed to recover financially from his duties of entertaining visiting royalty, he arranged to give lectures, for which he was paid, and claimed it was either that, "steal or resign." On a train to one speaking engagement, he met a man who remarked of the weather, "Mighty bad day for business."

Marshall asked, "What's your line?"

"Automobile accessories. What's yours?"

"Distributing dope."

"I thought they wouldn't let you sell that stuff."

"But I have a special arrangement with the Administration for a short time."

Such a man would naturally have a word or two to say about being vice-president. He once compared the number-two person to "a man in a cataleptic state; he cannot speak; he cannot move; he suffers no pain; and yet he is perfectly conscious of everything that is going on about him." On being made a member of the board of regents of the Smithsonian Institute, Marshall remarked that he looked forward to the "opportunity to compare his fossilized life with the fossils of all ages."

His lighthearted approach could sometimes be used to calm savage senatorial tempers. Once, while he was presiding over a particularly heated exchange about the Versailles Treaty, Marshall interrupted to read a letter from a father who wanted a senator to pick a name for his new son. He had written that "the man who will give the baby the biggest prize can have the name . . . Mr. Marshall, see what you can do for me."

Marshall's most difficult period as vice-president came when Wilson suffered a stroke, in 1919. When told of the extent of the president's illness by Baltimore *Sun* reporter J. Fred Essary, Marshall "sat speechless, staring at his hands [and] never even looked up." Despite the urgings of some, Marshall refused to step in to the president's place, saying that this would be unconstitutional and could lead to civil war. He felt it would be a tragedy for him and the people if he had to be acting-president when there were so many who knew more about it than he did. He would not "seize the place and then have Wilson, recovered, come around and say, 'Get off, you usurper.' "

Once, while speaking at an out-of-town engagement, he was handed a note by a breathless policeman that said that Wilson had died. A shaken Marshall told his audience that he had to rush back to Washington to assume the duties of the executive office. On returning to his hotel, he found, to his relief and embarrassment, that the note had been a hoax.

Marshall became the first vice-president to be reelected since John Calhoun, but he was not unhappy to give it up in 1921. His wire to his (Republican) successor, Calvin Coolidge, read: "Please accept my sincere sympathy."

Calvin Coolidge

"Silent Cal"

REPUBLICAN
IN OFFICE: 1921–1923
PRESIDENT: WARREN G. HARDING

Calvin Coolidge remains today pretty much what he appears to have set out to be when alive: an enigma. This he achieved by saying very little and allowing current events to run their own course. Was he, as some Republicans asserted, "as cold and as dumb as an oyster," or was "Silent Cal" possessed of deep wisdom? Theodore Roosevelt's sharp-tongued daughter, Alice, described Coolidge's poker face as that of a "man weaned on a pickle." In any case, this stone-faced Vermont-bred man with his frugal ways and honest eighteenth-century values was just what the country needed in the Jazz Age of the twenties: "the shelter of a great rock in a weary land," as one admirer put it.

Editor and journalist Walter Lippmann once thought he had the mystery figured out, writing that "Mr. Coolidge's genius for inactivity is developed to a very high

CALVIN COOLIDGE

(Artist: Dwight Case Sturges. National Portrait Gallery, Smithsonian Institution, Washington, D.C.)

point. It is far from being an indolent inactivity. It is a grim, determined, alert inactivity which keeps Mr. Coolidge occupied constantly . . ."

He may not have had a naturally forceful personality, but Coolidge certainly seemed to have a lot of luck politically—perhaps because he was born on the Fourth of July. He was successful in nineteen of the twenty elections he entered, and was so conspicuously fortunate that one of his friends said, upon Cal's becoming vice-president, "I wouldn't give two cents for Warren Harding's life."

In 1919, the first year Coolidge was governor of Massachusetts, the Boston police went out on strike. His handling of this crisis put him in the limelight, for at this time the country was exhibiting a fair amount of paranoia in the wake of the Russian Revolution, and all strikes were thought to be communist plots. The city of Boston fired the striking policemen, and when union leader Samuel Gompers petitioned the governor to reinstate them, Coolidge replied, "There is no right to strike against the public safety by anyone, anywhere, any time." This made him a national hero.

At the 1920 Republican convention, Massachusetts senator Henry Cabot Lodge led a group determined to put into the White House a man who would yield to the legislative branch while in office. The nomination went to Senator Warren G. Harding of Ohio. (Editor and satirist H. L. Mencken pegged Harding as a man who "intellectually seems to be merely a benign blank . . .") When it was proposed to California senator Hiram W. Johnson that he be Harding's running mate, Johnson sneered: "We're living in a day of strange events, but none so strange as that I should be considered second to Senator Harding."

The Republican leaders then decided to arrange it that Wisconsin senator Irvine H. Lenroot would be the vice-presidential candidate. In a moment of careless self-confidence, however, the convention chairman recognized a rebellious Oregon delegate, who promptly placed Coolidge's name in nomination. In spite of Senator Lodge's feeling that any man who lived in a two-family house (as Coolidge did) was not suitable for high office, Coolidge was nominated in a landslide. The eighty-six-year-old former senator Chauncey DePew later told him, "I have been present at every Republican Convention beginning with 1856, and I have never seen such a spontaneous and enthusiastic tribute as the vote for you for vice-president." When the convention telephoned Coolidge in Boston with the news, he turned to his wife and said, "Nominated for Vice President." She said, "You're not going to take it, are you?" He replied, "I suppose I'll have to."

The Republicans ran their candidates against the Democrats' Ohio governor James M. Fox and Assistant Secretary of the Navy Franklin Delano Roosevelt, Harding pontificating from his front porch in Marion, Ohio, and Coolidge speaking to whatever audiences were deemed likely to appreciate his clipped Yankee twang. At least one newspaper felt that the Republican ticket had a "Kangaroo character [stronger in the hind quarters], with a colorless candidate and a platform which says anything or nothing." The *New York Times* editorialized that "Coolidge for Vice-President really shines by comparison with the head of the ticket."

Handsome, white-haired Harding and "Fighting Quaker" Coolidge easily dominated the Democrats at the polls. Women, who were voting for the first time in 1920, may have had something to do with the results. Like the rest of the nation, they longed for a return to "normalcy."

President Harding said he thought the vice-president "should be more than a mere substitute in waiting," and invited Coolidge to sit in on cabinet meetings. Cal sat in his usual taciturn manner, not speaking unless directly addressed. He later claimed that the experience was invaluable for his succession to the presidency. He also displayed a cool head when presiding over the Senate. During one particularly raucous session, when urged to use the gavel to restore order, he laconically responded, "Yes I shall if they get excited."

Socially, too, the vice-president fulfilled his duties by accepting frequent dinner invitations, admitting to one hostess that he "had to eat somewhere." Not surprisingly, Coolidge was not a great conversationalist at table. A frustrated dinner partner once bet Coolidge that she could get him to say more than two words—to which he snapped, "You lose."

By 1923, revelations of the criminal activities of Harding's Ohio "gang" in the Teapot Dome scandal and other politico-economic shenanigans were taking their toll on the president's health. He sought to escape his troubles on the other side of the country with an "inspection trip" to Alaska. But it was too late. Death came to him in a San Francisco hotel room, the result, according to the rumors of the day, of either a broken heart, ptomaine poisoning, murder (by his wife), or suicide.

Coolidge was asleep at his father's farm in Plymouth Notch, Vermont, when the news came at about one in the morning of August 3. He dressed, was sworn in by his father, a justice of the peace, and then went back to bed. When Coolidge was later asked about his feelings at the time, he replied, "I thought I could swing it."

As president, Coolidge lived up to his philosophy that "the business of America is business," and would do nothing to interfere with the ventures of the capitalists he so admired. And he stuck with what he considered the most effective method of governing, as he described it to his secretary of commerce, Herbert Hoover: "If you see ten troubles coming down the road, you can be sure that nine will run into the ditch before they reach you and you have to battle with only one of them."

Charles Gates Dawes

Asleep at the Switch

REPUBLICAN
IN OFFICE: 1925–1929
PRESIDENT: CALVIN COOLIDGE

And when his statue is placed on high,
Under the dome of the Capitol sky . . .
Be it said, in letters both bold and bright:
O, Hell an' Maria, he has lost us the fight!

This stanza of poetic parody was read into the *Congressional Record* by Senator George Norris of Nebraska after an incident that Vice-President Dawes would have preferred forgotten. In the first week of his 1925–1929 term in office, President Coolidge was sending the Senate his list of appointees, one of whom was Charles B. Warren for attorney general. It promised to be a close count and likely to require Dawes's tie-breaking vote. Dawes, accustomed to a refreshing nap in the afternoon, was assured that the wrangling would go on for hours and

CHARLES G. DAWES
(Photographers: Underwood and Underwood. Collections of the Library of Congress)

that he would have time to return to his hotel for a rest. That may have been the signal for the Democrats to bring things to a head, with the result that there was a tie vote of 40 for and 40 against. The Republicans frantically tried to stall the proceedings until the vice-president could return, but by the time his taxi had rushed him to the Senate and he had sprinted down the halls it was too late. A Democrat switched to a No vote and the appointment was rejected.

Dawes blamed the incident on his "inexperience with the explosive nature" of the Senate, but won no forgiveness from the infuriated Coolidge, who already had good reason to feel antagonistic toward his number-two man. During the inauguration ceremony, Dawes had managed to steal whatever thunder Silent Cal could generate with his speech on the economy by giving a harangue on the dangers of the filibuster rule. Dawes's attempts to reform senatorial procedures prompted Senator Joseph Robinson of Arkansas to remark: "Dawes showed as little knowledge of the Senate's rules as he did good taste—not quite as little but nearly."

As loquacious as Coolidge was terse, Dawes was inclined to jump in rather than allow events to drift. Even before the inauguration, the outspoken Dawes had managed to anger Coolidge by sending him a letter stating that he would not sit in on cabinet meetings, claiming that it involved "a wrong principle." To make matters worse, he took his letter to the press. Since Dawes had not even been asked to participate, he effectively removed the initiative from the president, who should have made the decision and who obviously disagreed.

That was three strikes for Dawes—who could not have been more different from Coolidge anyway.

The vice-president, a wealthy businessman from Illinois, had never held an elective office before. An early admirer of the Hanna-McKinley faction of the Republican party, Dawes successfully ran McKinley's presidential campaign in Illinois in 1896. Six years later, Hanna and McKinley were dead and so were Dawes's chances for elective office; he lost a bid for the Senate in 1902 and didn't run for office again for twenty-two years.

In 1917, the fifty-two-year-old Dawes enlisted for active duty in France and was assigned to the army's purchasing department under General John Pershing. A year later, he was a brigadier general and the head of the department. After the war, a congressional committee called Dawes up before it to explain some of the high prices he had paid for supplies, and it was from this that he earned his nickname. Exasperated by the pettiness of the questions, Dawes finally burst out: "I'd have paid horse prices for sheep if the sheep could have hauled artillery. . . . Hell and Maria, we weren't trying to keep a set of books, we were trying to win the war!" From then on, he was "Hell and Maria" Dawes to an appreciative nation.

He did a very efficient job as Harding's director of the Bureau of the Budget, and then in 1923 headed a commission investigating the possibilities of Europe's economic recovery after the war. Although he worked in collaboration with lawyer and corporation executive Owen D. Young, the final result became known as the

Dawes Plan, for which he was awarded the Nobel Peace Prize in 1925.

The Republicans in 1924 nominated former Illinois governor Frank O. Lowden for vice-president in spite of his repeated protestations, and he became one of the few politicians to turn down the nomination. So it went to "Hell and Maria" Dawes. Will Rogers once asked Coolidge, who was obviously displeased with the convention's choice, why he did not choose to have a say in the nomination. To this Coolidge modestly replied, "Nobody told them in 1920 and they did all right."

"Cautious Cal Coolidge" and "Charging Charlie Dawes" did not have to work very hard against the badly splintered Democrats, whose nominees were John W. Davis, former congressman and ambassador, and Charles W. Bryan, William Jennings's brother and governor of Nebraska. Dawes did most of the speaking, since the president was in mourning for the death of his young son. Dawes campaigned vigorously against the "sinking sands of Socialism," but was never popular with labor groups; they were worried about the anti-unionism of an organization he had founded in 1923: the Minute Men of the Constitution.

It is certain that Coolidge would not have wanted the same vice-president for a second full term, but that was beside the point after he announced in 1927 that he did not choose to run for president in 1928. President Herbert Hoover later appointed Dawes his ambassador to the Court of St. James, where he became very popular with the reserved British for his outspokenness.

Dawes may not have been too disappointed not to be

renominated, for as he once told Kentucky senator Alben W. Barkley: "Barkley, this is a helluva job! I can do only two things: one is to sit up here and listen to you birds talk, without the privilege of being able to answer you back. The other is to look at the newspapers every morning to see how the President's health is!"

Charles Curtis

"Alexander Throttlebottom"

REPUBLICAN
IN OFFICE: 1929–1933
PRESIDENT: HERBERT HOOVER

The blood of the Kaw Indian tribe flowed sluggishly through the arteries of our thirty-first vice-president, Charles Curtis. It is unfortunate—since he was the only vice-president to claim ancestry with the original natives of America—that Curtis has not gone down in history as a great politician. He was an ultraconservative for whom "the trinity meant the Republican Party, the high protective tariff and the Grand Army of the Republic." He was, however, the inspiration for a character in the long-running Broadway show *Of Thee I Sing.* Alexander Throttlebottom was the shy, bumbling, ineffectual vice-president in the 1931 musical, elected because "They put a lot of names in a hat and he lost." Throttlebottom constantly worried that his mother would find out about his lowly job.

Young Charles, whose own mother had died when he

CHARLES CURTIS
(Collections of the Library of Congress)

was three, divided his childhood years between two sets of grandparents. He spent three years living on a Kaw reservation in Kansas, where he learned to ride horses well enough to earn money as a jockey at local fairs. He started school when he was nine years old, and did well enough to be admitted to the bar at twenty-one. Four years later, he won his first elective office, which was the beginning of a political career lasting almost five decades, including twenty years in the U.S. Senate.

Like Throttlebottom, Curtis considered the vice-presidency a "lowly" job, and would have preferred to be president. At the 1928 Republican convention, he garnered only 64 votes to the 837 votes of Herbert Hoover, who had never held elective office. Curtis was named to the number-two spot in an effort to placate farmers, whose slogan was "Anyone but Hoover," (because of his opposition to farm subsidies during his time as Secretary of Commerce). Prior to the convention, Curtis had worked against Hoover, asking, "Why should we nominate a man for whom we will have to apologize throughout the campaign," but after his nomination Curtis said he was glad to run with an "old friend." They ran against New York's Catholic governor Alfred E. Smith and Senator Joseph T. Robinson of Arkansas.

Political writer Oswald Villard called Curtis "the apotheosis of mediocrity" and "as faithful and devoted to his party as he is dull and dumb." It was conceded that the country was fortunate in the good health of Hoover, because the succeeding president could have been a man whose politics were, as one co-worker said, "always purely personal. Issues never bothered him."

Will Rogers, another part-Indian, who was covering

the convention, wrote: "The Republican Party owed Curtis something, but I didn't think they would be so low-down as to pay him that way. He used to be floor walker of the Republican Party on the Senate floor. Now he will be timekeeper." H. L. Mencken pegged the team "Lord Hoover and the Injun" and termed Curtis's speaking style "half Choctaw and half windmill."

To understand how such an uninspiring person as Curtis could have been elected to high office so many times, it is important to bear in mind that he and his assistant and half-sister, Dolly Curtis Gann, actually kept complete dossiers ("a short biography of each voter . . . all the facts we could gather") on his most influential constituents. Not many of these would be comfortable voting against a national representative who seemed to know so much about them.

Once he was vice-president, Curtis did not seem to mind that Hoover had no use for him. He relished the trappings of high office and was delighted with the small amount of work required of him. But he was no more Mister Nice Guy, and insisted that even his friends call him Mr. Vice-President. On one occasion, he refused to shake hands with some black constituents who had stopped by his office.

Curtis, a widower, enlisted his half-sister, Dolly, to serve as his official hostess, and together they performed at least one important service during the time of the Great Depression. Their social antics distracted and amused an anxious nation. Dolly's exact position in Washington society was a matter of debate; there were those, including the formidable Alice Roosevelt Longworth, wife of the Speaker of the House, who did not agree that a sister rated the same seating privileges as a wife at state dinners. The issue, which spread to include ambassadors and several branches of the government, became an almost-too-easy topic for the satirists of the day. The depression, which would soon add many in the Republican party to the lists of the unemployed, did not appear to be a major inconvenience for either Charles or Dolly. In an ill-timed public utterance, she once claimed that it was already over, leading one newspaper to issue the marvelously ironic headline, "Dolly Calls It Off."

Hoover and Curtis were not keen to run with each other again in 1932, but the Republican party was not going to sacrifice two innocents against F.D.R., and the old team was renominated. During their campaign, Curtis continued with his faux pas: once, speaking before a less-than-enthusiastic group of unemployed, he told them they were just "too damn dumb" to understand the depression.

The tenure of Charles Curtis marked the end of the Throttlebottom vice-presidents. After him, the office was occupied, with one exception, by men who were intelligent or experienced enough in their own right to succeed to the presidency.

John Nance Garner

"Cactus Jack"

DEMOCRAT

IN OFFICE: 1933–1941

PRESIDENT:

FRANKLIN DELANO ROOSEVELT

Texan "Cactus Jack" Garner made the ultimate sacrifice for his party when he accepted the vice-presidential nomination and "gave up the second most important job in the government for one that didn't amount to a hill of beans." After spending thirty years in the House of Representatives, Garner had realized his primary ambition—to become Speaker—in 1931, just one year before the Democratic convention that made him Franklin Roosevelt's running mate.

Garner had gone to the convention a potential presidential candidate in possession of 90 sure votes: 46 as the favorite son of Texas and 44 of California's, thanks to the machinations of publishing magnate William Randolph Hearst. New York's governor, Franklin Roosevelt, had gone in strong for the presidency, but after 3 ballots still could not get the necessary two-thirds, and

JOHN N. GARNER
(Photographers: Underwood and Underwood. Collections of the Library of Congress)

his support seemed to be wavering. Garner saw his chance for martyrdom and took it. He released his votes to F.D.R., but not before his unhappy fellow Texans demanded that Garner be made the vice-presidential nominee.

In discussing his options, Garner remarked to his friends that he had "something of a reputation as a trader, and that reputation would not be helped any by trading the second most important office in the nation for one which, in itself, is almost wholly unimportant." Why did he do it? The way he told it was that "the country needs the Democratic Party in power at this time . . ." Remembering the dissensions and rancor of the 1924 convention—which had left the party too splintered to win—Garner made his choice to avoid "so bitter a contest that chances of winning an election would have ceased to exist."

Garner's life as a career Democrat began when he was elected judge of Uvalde County, Texas, in 1895. In this capacity, when it came time to form a new district for the state, he drew up the boundaries and had himself elected the national representative of an area larger than Pennsylvania. After his first election, he seldom bothered to campaign; his constituents knew what he would do for them and just kept sending him back. Garner made few speeches and introduced few bills in Congress, preferring to accomplish his aims over poker games with speaker Joseph Cannon and other political cronies.

Outspoken against Prohibition, women's suffrage, and the Ku Klux Klan, Garner did not mince words when it came to the vice-presidency either. He said it was "not worth a bucket of warm spit." In a more refined mood, he reflected: "A great man may be vice-president but he can't be a great vice-president, because the office in itself is unimportant." And yet Garner went far to disprove this statement by becoming one of our most effective and hardworking vice-presidents. He sat in at cabinet meetings, acted as liaison in seeing that Roosevelt's New Deal bills were passed, and was the first vice-president to be sent abroad on official business—to the Philippines, Japan, and Mexico. But he drew the line at the socializing a vice-president usually falls prey to, saying the hours between six in the evening and seven in the morning were his own.

To get the necessary votes for one of Roosevelt's bills in the Senate, Garner would sometimes amble down and sit with a doubtful senator. Or he would invite some of them back to his office for an informal session with bourbon and branch water to "strike a blow for liberty." When Louisiana senator Huey Long baited him from the floor by asking how he should vote if he was half for and half against a bill, Garner told him: "Get a saw and saw yourself in two; that's what you ought to do anyhow."

Roosevelt and Garner were overwhelmingly reelected in 1936—defeating the Republicans' Kansas governor Alfred ("Alf") Landon and Chicago publisher-politician Frank Knox—but their relationship began to sour. The conservative vice-president became alarmed by the continuing New Deal programs: deficit spending, the politics of personality, and White House interference in congressional races. He advised F.D.R. to slow down and "let the cattle graze"; but the president was on a roll and was not about to let anyone interfere with his plans—and these included some for the Supreme Court.

In 1937, Roosevelt shocked Garner and the Congress with his plan to "pack the court" by adding six new justices who would be more in tune with his ideas than the conservatives then sitting, who were overruling some of his favorite programs. Crusty Cactus Jack left no doubt about his feelings on the issue by walking through the Senate halls holding his nose and giving the thumbs-down sign. He then went home for a vacation, saying that his ears were "buzzing and ringing" with the Court battle. He would not return in spite of the president's pleas and complaints that this was "a fine time for him to jump ship." The schism widened when Roosevelt arranged to have his man Alben Barkley made Senate majority leader and when he would not agree to come down hard on labor strikes. Garner was no longer trusted not to leak cabinet-meeting business, so serious talks took place privately after the meetings, in what Garner called "prayer meetings."

Roosevelt began playing it coy on whether to run again in 1940, but he clearly felt it would be unwise for the country to change leadership with war imminent. Garner was vehemently opposed to a third term, insisting, "I wouldn't vote for my own brother for a third term."

Garner decided to run for president himself in 1940, with what must have been mixed emotions. After one visit to the White House, he had come away claiming, "I always thought of the White House as a prison, but I never noticed until today how much the shiny latch on the Executive office door looks like the handle on a casket." He need not have worried; he received only 61 votes to Roosevelt's 946.

Accepting the vice-presidency may well have been, as Garner said, the "worst damn-fool mistake" he ever made, but it was probably a godsend for F.D.R. As Speaker of the House, Garner would have been a powerful obstacle. As it was, in 1941, he went back to his forty-six-thousand-acre ranch, where he lived for another twenty-six years. The closest he ever came to being president had been in 1933, just before the inauguration, when crazed Italian bricklayer Giuseppe Zangara, shouting, "Too many people are starving to death," fired several shots at Roosevelt but missed and killed the mayor of Chicago.

Henry Agard Wallace

A Progressive

DEMOCRAT
IN OFFICE: 1941–1945
PRESIDENT:
FRANKLIN DELANO ROOSEVELT

Henry Wallace was such an unpopular choice for vice-president that he was advised not to give an acceptance speech at the convention for fear of the adverse reaction that would have been sure to follow. There were several reasons for his unpopularity but only one main factor in his nomination: Roosevelt insisted on it. And that was part of the problem: the delegates wanted to feel that they had some control over the selection of candidates, and resented being strong-armed by the man who was running for an unprecedented third term. The Republicans' nominees were Indianan lawyer and business executive Wendell L. Willkie and Oregonian senator Charles L. McNary.

Wallace was a Republican party dropout, so Democratic party pros also resented him as someone who had not really paid his dues. The Iowan provided a good geographical "balance" for the president, and politically he was as liberal domestically and as much an internationalist as his running mate. Roosevelt knew that he was weakening physically and wanted to insure the continuance of his programs if he did not survive the next four years. He was adamant on the subject of his running mate and would accept no other choice by the delegates, saying, in effect, "Well, damn it to hell, they will go for Wallace or I won't run, and you can jolly well tell them so."

Wallace would have been unpopular with a large segment of the convention merely because many of the other hopefuls were certain that the wily president had promised them the vice-presidency. But Wallace's streak of mysticism and interest in Eastern religions were also disturbing, as were his blunt statements against racism and any policy of appeasement toward the European fascists. Oklahoma governor Leon Phillips admitted that Wallace was his second choice. When asked who first choice would be Phillips replied, "Anyone—red, white, black, or yellow—that can get the nomination."

The enigmatic nominee was the son and grandson of agricultural experts and pioneers. He had followed his father as editor of the influential weekly magazine *Wallaces' Farmer* and then served as secretary of agriculture during F.D.R.'s first two terms. In that capacity, he urged farmers to slaughter 6,000,000 baby pigs in order to raise prices. For this advice he was labeled "The Greatest Butcher in Christendom." Wallace responded to the outcry by suggesting that perhaps people "sympathize more with little pigs which are killed than with

HENRY A. WALLACE
(Photographer: John Vachon. Collections of the Library of Congress)

full-grown hogs" and "think that farmers should run a sort of old-folks home for hogs." The demise of the little porkers, in fact, meant millions of pounds of meat for the poor and a price rise of 50 percent for the farmers.

As vice-president, Wallace often napped while presiding in the Senate, and made little effort to endear himself to its members. Missouri senator Harry S. Truman would later claim: "In the past four years, I doubt if there are a half a dozen Senators all told who have been in the Vice-President's office."

Roosevelt had bigger plans for Wallace than his use as congressional liaison man. He sat in the cabinet meetings and was sent abroad—to Mexico, Russia, and China—making a favorable impression because of his attempts at fluency in various languages. His most important post, however, was as chairman of the Economic Defense Board, later the Board of Economic Warfare, which was in charge of procuring war materials. This probably made him the most powerful and influential vice-president to date, and so naturally also increased the number of his enemies. Chief among these was Secretary of Commerce Jesse H. Jones, who happened to head a board with overlapping responsibilities. A harassed president was finally forced to eliminate both boards in order to end "acrimonious public debate."

As it became clearer that the president, though failing in health, would win a fourth term, efforts to rid the ticket of Wallace—that "wild radical . . . visionary idealist and . . . merchant of globaloney"—intensified. Party kingmakers convinced Roosevelt that "the boomerang-throwing mystic from the place where the tall corn grows" was too controversial and should be replaced by

Harry Truman, the junior senator from Missouri. Meanwhile, the now determined-to-win Republican party placed New York governor Thomas E. Dewey and Ohio governor John W. Bricker on the 1944 ticket. Democratic National Chairman Robert E. Hannegan would later express his party's satisfaction with the election results when he stated, "When I die, I would like to have one thing on my headstone—that I was the man who kept Henry Wallace from becoming President of the United States."

If Wallace had won a second term as vice-president and then become president, following Roosevelt's death on April 12, 1945, postwar diplomacy would surely have taken a different direction than it did, because he was quite enamored of Communist Russia. He felt it was a kindred spirit with the United States in fighting fascism, including those American capitalists who, as "midget Hitlers . . . continually attack labor." It was this pro-Soviet stand that in 1946 led to his ouster as secretary of commerce from Truman's cabinet. Secretary of State James F. Byrnes complained that Wallace made it difficult for the Russians to take his own hard line seriously.

Two years later, Wallace formed and headed his own Progressive party. He discovered that there were 1,157,140 people, some of whom were not communists, who thought he should be president—but not quite enough for an election win. Eleanor Roosevelt may have summed up his problem as a vote-getter when she said, "Mr. Wallace is perhaps too idealistic—and that makes him a bad politician."

Harry S. Truman

"Give 'Em Hell, Harry"

DEMOCRAT
IN OFFICE: 1945
PRESIDENT:
FRANKLIN DELANO ROOSEVELT

By 1944, it was obvious to anyone who saw him that twelve years in the White House had taken their toll on President Roosevelt, and it seemed unlikely that he would survive another term. This meant that the vice-presidential nomination took on an importance that it had never before known, and—at least in the glow of revisionist history—the Democratic party pros made a good choice.

Twenty years after leaving the presidency in 1953, Harry Truman attained a popularity unaccorded him during his terms in office. Disgusted with the Watergate revelations, people paid homage to Truman's modesty, frankness, loyalty, and outspokenness and drove around with bumper stickers saying "America Needs You, Harry Truman." This would have been very satisfying to the little "failed haberdasher" from Mis-

HARRY S. TRUMAN
(Artist: Augustus Vincent Tack. National Portrait Gallery, Smithsonian Institution, Washington, D.C.)

souri, who had died a year earlier. Americans were not so sanguine when they woke up on April 13, 1945, and realized they had a new president.

The differences between the charismatic wartime leader and his sixty-year-old bespectacled successor were striking. Unlike F.D.R., Truman had come up in the world the hard way, trying his hand at banking, farming, and shopkeeping before turning to politics as a means to make a living. It was one of the friends Truman had made in the army in World War I who introduced him to Tom Pendergast, boss of the Democratic party machine in Missouri.

Pendergast soon saw to it that Truman, who was not a college graduate, was elected county judge, a job that involved handing out public contracts. It was here that Harry first publicly demonstrated his honesty by always going with the lowest bidders. A decade later, he was ready for something more, such as county collector or even congressman, but Pendergast had only one slot open: the U.S. Senate. Pendergast offered this to Truman either to get rid of him, to have a friend in power, or because there was no one else. Once elected, Senator Truman worked hard for the New Deal and proved himself independent of the Pendergast machine. This was fortunate, because Pendergast himself was soon in jail for bribery and fraud. Truman had to work very hard for a second term, and for his gutsy fight he won a standing ovation on reentering the Senate. During the war years, he came to national prominence as chairman of the Senate Special Committee to Investigate the National Defense Program, known simply as the Truman Committee, whose thorough, nonpartisan work saved the government $15,000,000,000 in its exposure of graft and overspending. It also made Roosevelt sit up and take notice of Truman.

Harry's views on vice-presidents were colorful. He claimed they "were about as useful as a cow's fifth teat" and just sat around "hoping for a funeral." But there were many who, through a process of elimination, were narrowing in on Truman for just that office as the 1944 convention approached. Vice-President Wallace was too mystical, Supreme Court Justice William O. Douglas was too liberal, presidential assistant James Byrnes could not carry labor, but Truman had no enemies. Democratic leader Robert Hannegan and others wheedled and pressured a president too weak and preoccupied to resist, and finally got him to put something in writing. The note originally had said that he would be happy with either Douglas or Truman on the ticket, but mysteriously, the names were somehow switched around so that Truman's came first, before the delegates saw it.

Truman frustrated Hannegan by not actively campaigning for the job at the convention. In fact, he was planning to make the nominating speech for Byrnes. Hannegan finally sat him down in his hotel room while he telephoned to Roosevelt, who was on the West Coast. The president's booming voice came through loud enough for Truman to hear him ask, "Bob, have you got that fellow lined up yet?"

Hannegan replied, "No, he is the contrariest Missouri mule I've ever dealt with."

The president said, "Well, you tell him if he wants to break up the Democratic Party in the middle of a war, that's his responsibility"—and hung up.

An incredulous Truman told the group around him, "Well, if that is the situation I'll have to say yes, but why the hell didn't he tell me in the first place?"

Truman's eighty-three days as vice president were filled with social affairs and a few cabinet meetings but nothing of substance. No one bothered to sit him down and explain about the Manhattan Project or the agreements worked out with the Allies or anything else that might have helped the man who had, after all, been chosen as F.D.R.'s heir apparent. When Truman did succeed, he felt as though "the moon, the stars, and all the planets had fallen on me."

As president, Truman scored incredibly low on the Gallup popularity polls and convinced nearly everyone, including most of the press, that he could never be elected president in 1948. Many underestimated him as an undignified, piano- and poker-playing user of coarse language: the man who dropped the atomic bomb; the man who threatened the railroad unions with an army takeover; and later as the man who fired the popular Korean War hero General Douglas MacArthur. South Carolina Senator Strom Thurmond spoke for many disgruntled Southerners when he agreed that Truman was only taking Roosevelt's course on civil rights, then added, "But Truman means it."

Truman was also in on the beginnings of the NATO European alliance; the Marshall Plan, which kept postwar Europe alive; the Truman Doctrine, which kept the Soviets out of Greece and Turkey; and a strong civil rights program. But it was his almost thirty-thousand-mile whistle-stop train tour in 1948 that exposed enough people to his basic good qualities, so that he was able to confound most of the experts—and a complacent renominated Tom Dewey, paired with California governor Earl Warren—and win the election.

Today most historians rank Truman as one of the near-greats as a president, in part because of how hard he worked to "grow into" the office and in part because of his style, exemplified when he said, "I never did give anybody hell. I just told the truth, and they thought it was hell."

Alben William Barkley

"The Veep"

DEMOCRAT
IN OFFICE: 1949–1953
PRESIDENT: HARRY S. TRUMAN

Vice-President Alben Barkley would make the record books on three counts: he was the oldest vice-president, the only one to marry in office, and the last to be born in a log cabin. And though it has not been conclusively proven, he was probably the best hog caller ever to preside over the Senate.

The son of a Kentucky tenant tobacco farmer, Barkley worked his way through college and law school and was a natural for politics because of his inclinations to give a speech whenever he saw "as many as six persons assembled together." After serving as a county prosecuting attorney and then judge, he entered the U.S. House of Representatives in 1913. He stayed there for fourteen years before moving up to the Senate for twenty-two more years, and becoming majority leader.

From the time he entered the Senate, his name was

ALBEN W. BARKLEY
(Collections of the Library of Congress)

being mentioned for the vice-presidency, but by the time it was taken seriously Barkley was already counted out as too old. In 1948, he was seventy and still did not feel too old. Truman's first choice for the nomination, Justice William O. Douglas, turned it down. Another name mentioned was Eleanor Roosevelt's. Truman said that he wouldn't mind having her on the ticket, but there were few others willing to take a woman candidate seriously. At the convention, Barkley made his willingness for the nomination known, but added that "it will have to come quick. I don't want it passed around so long it is like a cold bisquit." To make sure there was no doubt about his interest, he telephoned Truman to tell him that he wanted to be his running mate. The president, glad not to have to look any further, replied, "Why didn't you tell me you wanted to be vice-president?"—and that was it. As convention keynote speaker, Barkley gave a rousing oration that had the delegates clamoring for his nomination; as chairman of the Committee to Notify the Vice-presidential Nominee, he had little to do.

It may have been because the delegates—and most of the rest of the Democratic party—were so depressed about chances of winning the election that they were willing finally to put the old man on the ticket, but his campaign schedule would have tired many younger people. Traveling by chartered plane, Barkley spoke in thirty-six states and flew 150,000 miles.

Truman, determined to give his vice-president some real responsibility, requested that Congress pass a statute making him a member of the National Security Council, where Barkley actively participated in policymaking decisions, such as the United States' intervention in Korea and the recall of General Douglas MacArthur.

Almost everyone loved the affable, good-humored vice-president—from his grandson, who coined the affectionate nickname "Veep" for him, to the senators over whom he presided. He even managed to find some amusement in their tedious speech-making. When the senator from Tennessee complained that another senator had yawned during a speech from the floor, Barkley ordered that "the yawn of the Senator from Illinois will be stricken from the record." The seventy-one-year-old widower Barkley also found time to romance Jane Hadley, a widowed stenographer in her mid-thirties, and he would tune out the senators' speeches to write her love letters. They were married on November 18, 1949, to the delight of the country.

When Truman decided not to run again in 1952, Barkley announced his own intentions for the presidency, but labor leaders declared him too old and refused him the necessary support. The closest he ever came to being chief executive was in 1950, when two Puerto Rican nationalists tried to assassinate Truman while he was staying at Blair House.

For a while after leaving Washington, Barkley had a local television show called "Meet the Veep," but this was not stimulating enough for a man who had spent most of his life in public office, and he ran for the Senate again in 1954. He defeated his Eisenhower-backed opponent and returned to the capital as junior senator from Kentucky. In 1956, Barkley was asked to speak to the students of Washington and Lee University, who were conducting a mock convention. He told them how happy he was to be able to sit on the back row as a junior senator, and said, "I would rather be a servant in the House of the Lord than to sit in the seats of the mighty." He then fell back and died without ever knowing how warmly his last words were received.

One of Barkley's greatest assets had been his ability to tell a story, and he is given credit for the quintessential vice-presidential tale about the father of two sons: "One went to sea, the other was elected Vice-President; he never heard of either of them again."

Richard Milhous Nixon

"Tricky Dick"

REPUBLICAN

IN OFFICE: 1953–1961

PRESIDENT: DWIGHT D. EISENHOWER

Some people have claimed that a "New Nixon" appeared every few years, but there were really only two Nixons: one who was heartily hated and one who kept appearing on "Most Admired" lists.

There might have been just one Richard Nixon if he had not answered a newspaper ad in 1945 placed by some California Republican businessmen who were looking for someone to run against the state's liberal U.S. Representative, Jerry Voorhis. Nixon, a young conservative lawyer just out of the navy and looking for a career, appeared to be the perfect candidate. At that time, the easiest way to defeat a political opponent was to convince the voters that he or she was a communist sympathizer. And that was how, in 1946, Nixon defeated Voorhis, a man thought by many to be the "best congressman west of the Mississippi."

RICHARD M. NIXON
(Artist: Norman Rockwell. National Portrait Gallery, Smithsonian Institution, Washington, D.C.)

The new junior congressman from California was appointed to the House Un-American Activities Committee, where he heard Whittaker Chambers accuse ex-State Department employee Alger Hiss of being a communist. Hiss denied the accusation, and most of the credulous committee members were ready to drop the whole embarrassing issue. But Nixon would not let go. His bulldog tenacity eventually led to Hiss's perjury conviction and imprisonment. It also meant that Nixon would forever be anathema to a large influential group of intellectuals. His 1950 campaign for the Senate against Helen Gahagan Douglas involved even more virulent Red-baiting tactics than those used earlier, and once again Nixon won the election but alienated a large segment of the liberal press and population.

His successes in the Hiss case and his hard-hitting campaigns made Nixon the new young star in his party, and he was invited to speak before several organizations on the dangers of subversives and on corruption in the Democratic party. This exposure to thousands of fellow Republicans made him a natural for the list of vice-presidential possibilities in 1952. Once General Dwight D. Eisenhower had decided that he *was* a Republican and would run for president, Nixon went to the top of his list.

His youth (at forty, he would be the second-youngest vice-president since John Cabell Breckinridge) would balance Ike's years, and, more important, he could be counted on to do the down-and-dirty campaigning while Eisenhower perfected his fatherly image and his use of the famous grin. Everything went according to plan until September, when the New York *Post* ran the front-page headline "Secret Nixon Fund!"

This fund of about $18,000, raised by wealthy Californians to enable Nixon to pursue his politicking without dipping into his own meager salary, seemed easy enough to explain, but in a campaign that made much of the Democrats' supposed unethical practices it was a godsend to Nixon's enemies. Most of Eisenhower's advisers insisted that Nixon be dropped and a new candidate selected for the second spot on the ticket. Ike did not say much, one way or the other, until he told a group of reporters that the Republican ticket should be "as clean as a hound's tooth."

Now it was up to Nixon to prove that he was that clean; and arrangements were made for him to present his case to the nation on television. "Drop Nixon" telegrams and phone calls urging his resignation (including one from Thomas Dewey) poured in until just before he went on the air, but within hours of his final words—asking for public support—hundreds of thousands of people made it known that they were behind him. They apparently approved of the way he handled his personal finances (about which he gave every detail) and of the fact that his wife, Pat, wore a "respectable Republican cloth coat" and that, "regardless of what they say about it," the Nixons were going to keep their gift of a little cocker spaniel named Checkers. Then there was a tearful reunion with Ike, who told him, "You're my boy," and said he had completely "vindicated" himself. But for others "this mawkish ooze" and "financial striptease" meant that Nixon would always be a kind of sick joke, a "Tricky Dick," or a "McCarthy in a white collar."

Democratic Illinois governor Adlai Stevenson and Alabaman senator John J. Sparkman lost the election; as

Stevenson would, again, in 1956 with Tennessee senator Estes Kefauver as his running mate.

Unlike his predecessors, Nixon claimed to like being vice-president because it gave him the chance "to see the whole operation of the government and participate in its decisions." He was kept informed on issues, and traveled to fifty-four countries including the Soviet Union, where he held his own in the so-termed "Kitchen Debates" with Premier Nikita Khrushchev, and Venezuela, where he was spat on and in serious danger of having his car overturned. During three presidential illnesses, Nixon proved his calm and restraint, but a "Dump Nixon" movement began in 1956 that he overcame with only lukewarm support from Eisenhower.

During Nixon's 1960 presidential campaign—with former Massachusetts senator Henry Cabot Lodge II as running mate—Eisenhower was even more equivocal than usual, telling one group that he simply was not "able to believe that [Nixon] *is* presidential timber." When a reporter asked the outgoing chief what he thought Nixon's major decisions as vice-president had been, he replied, "If you give me a week, I might think of one." But it was the televised debates with John F. Kennedy that really ruined Nixon's chances. He lost his edge as the more experienced candidate when people saw how knowledgeable and self-assured Kennedy was. And, of course, Nixon looked stiff, exhausted, and unshaven next to Kennedy's forthright grace and handsomeness.

So Nixon lost in 1960 and then lost again in 1962 in the race for governor of California, when he seemed to write his own political obituary with his "You won't have

Nixon to kick around any more" speech to reporters. No one would then have believed in the Lazarus-like recovery that took him into the White House in 1968.

As the finale to a truly remarkable political career, Nixon became the first president to resign, forced out by the revelations of his part in the Watergate scandal, 1972–1974.

Lyndon Baines Johnson

"Landslide Lyndon"

DEMOCRAT
IN OFFICE: 1961–1963
PRESIDENT: JOHN F. KENNEDY

Lyndon Johnson had an ego that was a credit to the state of Texas—and ambition to go along with it. Put them together with a willingness to work eighteen-hour days and an uncanny knack of knowing who to use for what, and his rapid rise in politics should come as no surprise to anyone.

Johnson's father brought him up on the local machinations of the Democrat party; and in Texas, where a Republican was looked on as an alien, there was a lot to learn. Lyndon's first personal experience with politics, when he was just twenty-three, was his position as personal secretary to U.S. Representative Richard Kleberg, owner of the vast King Ranch.

Kleberg enjoyed the ceremonial aspects of his position and left the rest to Lyndon, who lost no time making himself popular with higher powers in Washington, including President Roosevelt. This began to worry Mrs. Kleberg, who, concerned that the young upstart might win her husband's seat, had Johnson fired. His new friends were looking out for him, however, and he was appointed to head one of F.D.R.'s New Deal projects: the National Youth Administration in Texas. Two years later, in 1937, Johnson was a congressman himself.

In 1940, Johnson lost a close race for the Senate against Governor "Pappy" O'Daniel, but picked up a valuable piece of advice from his supporter, President Roosevelt, who told him to next time "sit on the ballot box"; Texas politics were idiosyncratic, and ballots had a way of appearing or disappearing. During the next few years, L.B.J. kept his job in the House, bought an Austin radio station, which made him a millionaire, and spent a year in the navy. Then, in 1948, he had another chance at the Senate, and this time he did it right. First, he hired a helicopter to take him around the state; sometimes, if time was short, he would just broadcast his message down to the startled people on the ground. One rival said that "the *Johnson City Windmill* is the name of both the helicopter and its occupant." And this time Johnson sat on the ballot box—at least the one that held the necessary 87 votes and allowed him to win the primary. Despite the squawks of his opponents, "Landslide Lyndon" was now a senator.

Within a very short time, he became the Senate's Democratic leader and set about practicing what became known as "the treatment." This involved cajoling, compromising, bullying, and finally "the laying on of hands"—he was a great hugger and squeezer. But Johnson was not without critics, especially among the new

LYNDON B. JOHNSON
(Artist: Peter Hurd. National Portrait Gallery, Smithsonian Institution, Washington, D.C.)

younger senators who owed him nothing and resented his autocratic approach.

As the 1960 elections approached, and Johnson assessed his waning influence in the Senate, he began to consider running for the executive office, but he made some false assumptions on his chances for the presidency. Too many years of being completely wrapped up in the Senate's business led him to overestimate the ability of fellow senators to guarantee him votes. He also refused to enter the primaries, hoping that the other candidates would cancel each other out and that he would be the logical compromise candidate.

Probably his biggest mistake was in underestimating the well-financed Kennedy machine, which had been lining up delegate pledges for the past four years. Johnson thought L.B.J.–J.F.K. would be the perfect ticket, naturally listing himself first; he claimed that Kennedy was too young and that a president should have a little gray in his hair. When Johnson finally declared his candidacy just five days before the convention, it was already months too late.

As the vice-presidential discussions inevitably turned to Johnson, he declared that he "would not trade a vote for a gavel," but his thoughts must really have been running along a different track because he accepted Kennedy's offer with some alacrity—and probably with good reasons. In the first place, the vice-presidency would be a stepping-stone to national prominence, in which position he would not always have to worry about offending his Texas constituents. This would make him a logical presidential successor in eight years. His wife, Ladybird, urged him to take the nomination, knowing that the slower pace would be easier on a man who had already suffered one heart attack five years earlier. And his mentor, Speaker of the House Sam Rayburn, finally agreed to the nomination because Johnson would make the Democratic ticket strong enough to beat Rayburn's nemesis, Richard Nixon.

Labor was not happy with Johnson on the ticket; the liberals did not like him; the South was angry that he would run with a liberal Catholic; but Arizona senator Barry M. Goldwater may have had the strongest feelings, expressed in his telegram to Johnson: "I'm nauseated."

When someone asked Johnson why he would give up his prestige in the Senate for the vice-presidency, he asserted that "power is where power goes," but this was a miscalculation on his part: he had no power as vice-president, though not for lack of trying. He insisted on keeping a grand office suite known as the "Taj Mahal," and angered Democratic senators by asking to preside over their caucuses. He even sent Kennedy (who chose to ignore it) an executive order stating what he thought his prerogatives as vice-president should be, but Johnson just did not fit in with the bright young people then running the country.

Feeling rejected and useless, he contributed little at cabinet and National Security Council meetings or in legislative liaison work. He was happiest in his duties as head of the Space Agency and convinced Kennedy to let him ride down New York's Broadway with the first astronaut, John Glenn. When Johnson was on foreign tours, he was a very demanding guest (special beds and liquors were required) and his unstatesmanlike glad-handing could be embarrassing to embassy staff. Once, in Pakistan, he impulsively invited a camel driver to visit him in America, and to the relief of everyone, the visit of this poised and lyrical man, Bashir Ahmed, turned out to be a great public relations coup for Johnson.

Although President Kennedy would not allow anyone publicly to snipe at Johnson, the usual talk began of "dumping" the vice-president for the second term. We will never know if this would have happened because of the tragic assassination of Kennedy on November 22, 1963, in Dallas, Texas. Johnson went on to win a term of his own in 1964 and felt justifiably proud of the Great Society legislation he initiated, but even his ego could not stand up under the pressure and hatred engendered by the mounting war in Vietnam. He announced his decision not to run again in 1968 and went home to Texas, where he died four years later.

Hubert Horatio Humphrey

Minnesota Optimist

DEMOCRAT

IN OFFICE: 1965–1969

PRESIDENT: LYNDON B. JOHNSON

"I intend to set my aim at Congress. Don't laugh at me, Muriel . . . Oh Gosh, I hope my dreams come true . . ." So wrote twenty-four-year old Hubert Humphrey—in the nation's capital for the first time, leading a troop of Boy Scouts—to his fiancée back in Minnesota. She married him anyway, and he went on bubbling and gushing and wishing for the rest of his life.

His first wish was for a college education, and his father dropped him off at the University of Minnesota with the classic parental exhortation, "Good-bye. Good luck. Grow up." But autumn 1929 was not an easy time for anyone, and for financial reasons Hubert had to drop out after one year to work in his father's drugstore for the next eight years, before returning and graduating Phi Beta Kappa.

In 1945, Humphrey was elected mayor of Minneapolis and is credited with cleaning up corruption in the police department and sucessfully fighting organized crime in the city. Three years later, he gave a rousing speech at the Democratic National Convention that resulted in a strong civil rights plank being included in the Democratic platform and led to a walkout by some Southern delegates. He was also elected to the U.S. Senate.

Humphrey rushed in where angels and most junior senators feared to tread, but then he had a lot to say about a lot of things. Once, when he was asked about his willingness to talk about just about anything, he explained, "I do—I *like* every subject. I can't help it—it's just glands." His verbosity once caused his mentor, Lyndon Johnson, to sigh, "If I could just breed him to Calvin Coolidge . . ." Majority leader Johnson, who was a Southern conservative, claimed that liberal Humphrey's usefulness was in being a "link with the bomb throwers." Humphrey detractors have asserted that his close association with Johnson in the Senate resulted in Humphrey's liberal positions being watered down by accommodations. He once introduced a bill to make the Communist party illegal in the United States but sheepishly admitted later that it was "not one of the things I'm proudest of." He could be more proud of the consistency of his civil rights advocacy.

In 1956, his natural optimism led him to believe that a feeler put out by the presidential candidate meant that he would be Adlai Stevenson's running mate. When the nomination went to Tennessee senator Estes Kefauver, Hubert learned a little about not rushing out to buy a wardrobe for a job he didn't have.

HUBERT H. HUMPHREY
(Artist: Robert Templeton. National Portrait Gallery, Smithsonian Institution, Washington, D.C.)

It was his trip to the Soviet Union as a member of the Committee on Foreign Relations two years later that won Humphrey national recognition—and a cover on *Life* magazine. Not everyone could claim an eight-hour conversation with Nikita Khrushchev. Humphrey's pleasure at this acclaim bubbled over into openly wishing that he could be president in 1960. But his high spirits could not compete with the Kennedy organization and money, and his hopes were dashed early on with a loss in the West Virginia primary.

In late 1963, Johnson succeeded to the presidency and for the next year enjoyed enormous support and power as the country rallied behind him in its desire for order and continuity following the Kennedy assassination. There was no doubt that Johnson would be nominated for a full term, and few doubted that he would overwhelm the Republican candidate, Arizona senator Barry M. Goldwater (to be teamed with New York congressman William E. Miller), in November. This made the choice for the vice-presidency the most consuming question, and Johnson milked the situation for all its dramatic possibilities. Reporters panted after him as he dropped hint after name after conjecture. Every time he invited another possible candidate to his office, it made the headlines—as did his not-unexpected rejection of Attorney General Robert F. Kennedy.

Hubert Humphrey was the front-runner in the vice-presidential sweepstakes and wanted the nomination so badly that he was willing to agree to Johnson's terms—terms so demanding that Minnesota senator Eugene McCarthy eliminated himself from any consideration by the president. These included absolute loyalty and complete agreement with Johnson's decisions. Humphrey was also willing to put up with some cruel teasing by the chief executive, as when he leaned across someone at a dinner party to ask Hubert what he would think of Montana senator Mike Mansfield as vice-president.

This went on until convention time, when the president summoned Humphrey to the White House for a chat. Johnson told him that his research had shown that no president had ever gotten along with his vice-president, assured him that being number-two man was indeed a very difficult job, and said that Humphrey would have to curb his gregariousness and avoid headlines. All this was agreed to, and they set out to announce their joyous partnership to the delegates. For the first time, a presidential candidate introduced his running mate to the convention before the obligatory nominating speeches. Humphrey was very happy, maybe one of the few men who would still be happy after his running mate had said to him: "If you didn't know you were Vice President thirty days ago, maybe you're too stupid to be Vice President."

Humphrey must have had to swallow more bile in the days ahead, because Johnson could be a tormentor. He once insisted that a reluctant Humphrey prove he was as much a man as Robert Kennedy by shooting two deer on the L.B.J. ranch. Another time, Johnson had Humphrey put on some grotesquely huge ranching clothes and hat and then ride a spirited horse in front of a group of reporters.

Restraining his opinion on Johnson's Vietnam policy must have been Humphrey's greatest test of aquiescence. He was at one time ostracized from policymaking meetings because he objected to the timing of the bombing of North Vietnam. No deviation from administration policy would be tolerated even in cabinet meetings. It was this inability and/or unwillingness to speak out on important issues during four troubled years that, more than anything else, meant Humphrey's loss of the presidency to Richard Nixon in 1968. But, as Humphrey later ruefully explained, "Where you stand often depends on where you sit."

Spiro Theodore Agnew

Nolo contendere

REPUBLICAN
IN OFFICE: 1969–1973
PRESIDENT: RICHARD NIXON

With few exceptions (Aaron Burr, Teddy Roosevelt), vice-presidents do not become household words while they are in office. Vice-president Spiro Agnew, however, became well-known in America—but for all the wrong reasons: for insensitivity on the campaign trail, using terms such as "Polack" and "fat Jap"; for attacking war protestors and the media in inflammatory speeches while in office; and for being the first vice-president forced to resign in disgrace.

The selection of Agnew for the vice-presidency suggests that in 1968 the same old methods were being used to choose the person second in line to the nation's highest office. Nixon did not finally settle on this then-stranger to the nation because of his experience, knowledge, or ability, but because he was a "political eunuch." That is to say, the Maryland governor would not offend the South as

SPIRO T. AGNEW
(Collections of the Library of Congress)

New York's mayor John Lindsay would, and he would not panic the liberals as California governor Ronald Reagan would—just to mention two other vice-presidential possibilities that year. It was only when people got to know Agnew that they would be offended and panicky.

Agnew was one of those politicians who seemed to have risen solely by the yeast of luck. His performance as a student would have to be described as lackluster, his job experience as undistinguished. He was almost thirty-five before he became a practicing attorney, and never was a financial success in that field. Finally, in 1957, he pushed his way into an appointed position on the Baltimore County Council, helped immeasurably by the fact that he was one of the few registered Republicans in the area. Five years later, Agnew won his first elective office, as county executive.

In 1966, his luck held, when the dominant Maryland Democratic party splintered and nominated an embarrassing red-neck for governor and the Republican field narrowed to one: Agnew. He was forty-eight years old when elected and was thought to be a man with liberal or at least moderate tendencies, but his mouth was sending different signals regarding the unrest in the black community. After the Baltimore riots of 1968, he delivered such a stinging attack on the city's black leaders that most of them walked out of the meeting room.

New York governor Nelson A. Rockefeller was Agnew's first personal choice for president in 1968 (he thought that Nixon would make a "great secretary of state"), but Rocky embarrassed his ardent champion by dropping out of the race without informing him. Nixon filled the void. He, for some reason, considered Agnew a "real find," and wooed him with talk of the second spot on the ticket and then asked him to make the nominating speech at the Miami Beach convention.

Almost from the beginning of his campaign, this unknown man—far less familiar than Humphrey's running mate, Senator Edmund S. Muskie of Maine—polarized the nation. Millions of middle-class Americans (the Silent Majority), disturbed by the upheavals on streets and campuses, felt that this hounddog-faced Republican spoke for them. Others agreed with a Washington *Post* editor who wrote that Agnew's candidacy was "perhaps the most eccentric political appoinment since the Roman Emperor Caligula named his horse a consul." Agnew's image had gone from liberal as county executive, to moderate as governor, and to conservative as vice-presidential nominee—all without his having changed at all. He explained this by saying, "I've stayed still while literally thousands of people have rushed past me in a wild dash to the left." Those rushing people found reasons for dismay and disbelief in Agnew's campaign speeches, such as his claim that Hubert Humphrey was "squishy soft on Communism" or his explanation for not campaigning in the inner cities: "If you've seen one city slum, you've seen them all."

In spite of Nixon's praise of Spiro before the election and his promise of important duties as a domestic expert for the vice-president, once in office Agnew could not penetrate the White House and had no influence in the Senate. This left him with plenty of time for the speaker's circuit, where he perfected his polysyllabic and alliterative tirades against "an effete corps of impudent snobs" and "nattering nabobs of negativism" and that "tiny and closed fraternity of privileged men" in charge of the media. Nixon's staff began to think he had gone "off the reservation" in establishing his own constituency, and ridiculed him as a clown and a dummy—perceptions fueled by Agnew's penchant for slicing his tee shots into the galleries at golf tournaments.

When Agnew's rhetoric failed to prevent a Democratic takeover of Congress in 1970, a "Dump Agnew" movement began and might have succeeded if events had moved a little faster. In the fall of 1972, a Democratic ticket combining South Dakotan senator George S. McGovern and former ambassador and Peace Corps director Sargent Shriver failed to unseat Nixon and Agnew.

In 1973, it was disclosed that an investigation into corruption in Baltimore County had uncovered evidence of kickbacks, bribery, and extortion on the doorstep of the governor's mansion during Agnew's term there, as well as testimony of at least one payoff at the vice-president's office.

Agnew vociferously and persistently protested his innocence, at the same time trying either to claim executive clemency or to instigate the time-consuming impeachment proceedings. But there came a time when plea bargaining was the only way for him to stay out of jail. The vice-president promised to hand in his resignation, which was the primary concern of the prosecutors—especially Attorney General Elliot Richardson. Their greatest fear was that Agnew would succeed Nixon, then sinking in his own Watergate morass. In return, Agnew would not receive a prison sentence when he pleaded *Nolo contendere* (No contest) on October 10,

1973, to one charge of federal income tax evasion. Forty pages of evidence of additional criminal activities for which he was not formally charged were also read into the court record. He was fined $10,000 and given three years of unsupervised probation. On the same day, he handed in his resignation.

In later years, Agnew became a wealthy businessman, establishing homes on both coasts and enjoying the friendship of show business figures and the admiration of a host of people who still felt that he had spoken for them. Others, who saw injustice in the lightness of his sentence, consoled themselves with the thought that at least he never became president.

Gerald Rudolph Ford

"Mr. Clean"

REPUBLICAN
IN OFFICE: 1973–1974
PRESIDENT: RICHARD NIXON

Gerald Ford, known to some as "Nixon's Revenge," became the first beneficiary of the Twenty-fifth Amendment, when he was appointed to complete the term of Spiro Agnew. The president made a great production of announcing the appointment, arranging an East Room extravaganza and inviting an enthusiastic audience.

To most members of Congress, Ford seemed the perfect antithesis of the man who had resigned two days before; and he was one of them and had been for twenty-five years. It took less than two months for Congress to confirm him—after probing had confirmed that Ford had no financial funny business in his background and after extracting his promise that he would not run for president in 1976.

Ford was an unknown to most Americans outside his Michigan district but came across as honest and decent

GERALD R. FORD
(Collections of the Library of Congress)

in a government collapsing with corruption. Some cynics, however, persisted in finding fault with him. They criticized his conservative voting record against social reforms, his hard-line position on Vietnam, and his down-the-line party stand. Civil rights groups opposed him, and some critics were petty enough to bring up the time when, in a fit of pique for the rejection of two Nixon court appointees, he had tried to have Justice William O. Douglas impeached.

To Nixon, Ford was an old friend who would stand loyally by him and make no independent moves. In spite of what was said at the grand announcement, Nixon did not think that Ford would be considered acceptable as a replacement in the White House (Nixon once contemptuously asked Nelson Rockefeller if he could imagine Ford as President). But, in fact, Nixon became more expendable with Ford in the wings, and continuing disclosures of Watergate criminal activity finally forced the president's resignation.

The man who succeeded to the presidency on August 9, 1974, was born Leslie King but became Gerald Ford, Jr., by adoption. He was a University of Michigan football star, a Yale law school graduate, a lieutenant commander in the navy, and a Grand Rapids, Michigan, lawyer before being elected to Congress in 1948. And there he stayed, becoming House minority leader in 1964.

As vice-president, Ford made the usual objections, complaining, "I've got all the perks. But power? Power is what I left up there on Capitol Hill." Nixon was too immersed in Watergate to have much to do with his new vice-president, who devoted much of his time to cross-country speaking engagements. And it was difficult to keep track of his zigzagging position on Watergate. In one town, he would demonstrate his distance from the mess in Washington by calling for complete disclosures; in the next, he would declare that Nixon could not be involved, because he was "too smart for that." By the summer of 1974, however, it was becoming clear even to Gerald Ford that the emperor did indeed have no clothes and, when he learned of the "smoking gun" tape, Ford decided it would behoove him to say no more on the subject. Finally, on August 9, it was all over. Nixon made his maudlin farewells, and Ford became president.

For one month, there was euphoria in the country because of the open, modest man with his handsome family now in the White House. Then, on September 8, he spoiled it for many Americans when he announced a presidential pardon for Nixon on the grounds of compassion for the Nixon family as well as a need to shift national attention away from Watergate. Ford took this action without consulting the attorney general or anyone else who might advise against it—which was probably a mistake for someone already considered "not too bright."

Editorial writers immediately recalled Ford's ambiguous reply to a question on setting rules for White House ethics: "The code of ethics that will be followed," he had said, "will be the example I set." As Iowa's congressman H. R. Gross had once warned, "Jerry Ford will deal on anything, and don't forget it." When the pardon was announced, "deal" became the operative word in many suspicious minds.

His onetime fellow congressmen were appalled, and called him into a special session to explain the pardon to them. His press secretary, Jerry terHorst, resigned in protest at the unfairness of co-conspirators going to prison and draft dodgers being prosecuted, while Nixon went free. Ford insisted that there had been no deal and that a trial would be unnecessary because Nixon's acceptance of the pardon was an admission of guilt. But the president had lost his status as fair-haired boy for good. He probably had also lost any chance of election in his own right.

It seems that two weeks in the White House were all it took to make Ford change his mind about running for president in 1976, but he was unable to overcome his negative image. He was now seen as not too smart, insensitive, an old-time politician, indecisive as a leader, and a rather dull speaker. His biggest handicap may have been that he was the subject of ridicule. People loved to quote Lyndon Johnson, who once argued that Ford "can't chew gum and walk at the same time." Ford often mispronounced words ("geothermal" gave him a lot of trouble) and he once introduced Anwar Sadat of Egypt as the leader of Israel. One of his biggest blunders came in a debate with Jimmy Carter, when Ford made the incredible claim: "There is no Soviet domination of Eastern Europe, and there never will be under the Ford administration."

After Ford lost to Carter, he retired to Palm Springs, and to a life of golf and speaking tours. For social reasons and for their own safety, he and neighbor Spiro Agnew were said to avoid each other on the golf course.

Nelson Aldrich Rockefeller

The Richest Vice-President

REPUBLICAN

IN OFFICE: 1974–1977

PRESIDENT: GERALD FORD

The vice-presidency of Nelson Rockefeller was a strange interlude in American political history. He was, in effect, the appointee of an appointee who was the appointee of an impeachable president—a situation that would surely have dumbfounded the framers of the Constitution.

President Ford announced Rockefeller's appointment on August 20, 1974, but congressional hearings dragged on for four months, focused primarily on the financial dealings and possible conflicts of interest of one of the richest men in America. The most probing questions had to do with his gifts of several thousand dollars to friends and politicians. Some Americans, and congressmen, believed that the Rockefeller family controlled United States foreign policy through intermediaries such as Henry Kissinger, a Rocky protégé.

The magnitude of Rockefeller's wealth had always

NELSON A. ROCKEFELLER
(Collections of the Library of Congress)

been a drawback in his political aspirations—as well as one of his reasons for them. He once explained his ambitions by saying, "When you think of all I had, what else was there to aspire to?" He may have been speaking with ironic understatement when he told that his family was "quite fortunate in having adequate financial resources," but his perceptions of wealth sometimes appeared bizarre: he once spoke of middle-income people as being those in the one-hundred-thousand-dollar bracket. Rockefeller's background was what one might expect of a rich man, except that more emphasis was put on philanthropy.

Young Rockefeller went to the best schools, and in spite of suffering from dyslexia managed to graduate from Dartmouth a Phi Beta Kappa. He then went to work for the family business in New York City for a while. He made some kind of a name for himself when he asked Mexican painter Diego Rivera to eliminate a portrait of Lenin from his mural on one of the walls of Rockefeller Center. The artist quit, rather than comply, and all the Rivera murals were removed.

Rocky became familiar with some of the problems of Latin America when he visited the family's holdings in Venezuela, and on his return he took his ideas for improving U.S. relations with that part of the world to President Franklin Roosevelt. This led to his appointment as assistant secretary of state for Latin America in 1944, where he stayed until Truman fired him. President Eisenhower asked him back in 1953 to serve as under secretary of Health, Education and Welfare, but Rockefeller's proclivities for spending were too liberal for the administration, and he left to try for elective office.

In what seemed to many to be a hopeless attempt,

Rockefeller took on the Democratic incumbent, Averell Harriman, for governor of New York in 1958. Rocky grinned, shook hands, ate ethnic foods, and spent money all the way to the governor's mansion. The reviews for his fourteen years there were mixed. He almost doubled the number of state schools, built highways, and increased the number of parks, but his government-building complex in Albany was criticized as an "Instant Stonehenge" and "Rocky's Follies." Low marks were also given for his tax increases and for his handling of a revolt at Attica Prison in 1971. He refused the prisoners' demands that he meet with them personally, partly because the politician knew that if things did not work out, then "Nelson Rockefeller is there on world television as the man who failed." Instead, he sent the police in shooting, and dozens of inmates and hostages were killed.

Two years later, Rockefeller resigned as governor to form the National Commission on Critical Choices for Americans, a thinly disguised first step in what would be his final assault on the White House. He had come close to winning the presidential nomination in 1960, but had backed off when Nixon made such a strong showing in early primaries. He tried again in 1964, but could not buck the conservative Goldwater tide. At this point, too, there were many delegates who saw little voter appeal in a man who had just divorced his wife of more than three decades and mother of his five children and had hastily married a divorced woman who herself had lost custody of her five children. At the convention, he staunchly faced a booing, jeering mob that tried to drown him out, telling them, "Ladies and gentlemen, this is still a free country."

It was becoming clear that the rich, urbane Easterner had little in common with his party; but rather than leaving the Republicans, Rocky began moving to the right politically. Nevertheless, apparently he had not gone far enough or fast enough by 1968, because he again lost the nomination to Nixon.

The vice-presidency in 1974 must have seemed as near as the sixty-six-year-old Rockefeller would come to the White House, and he did not hesitate to accept the appointment, in spite of having once said that the vice-president was "standby equipment." He must also have known that he was not meant to be a number-two person —especially not to someone he probably considered inferior in many ways. But whatever hopes he may have had for the next election year were dashed when it became obvious that he was still poison to the party conservatives and would be a major drawback on a ticket that might have to consider the darling of the right wing: Ronald Reagan.

In discussing his letter of resignation from vice-presidential contention—which President Ford did not fight —Rocky said, "I eliminated the issue which was the basis of a lot of the squabble." Backing off seemed to give him a new sense of freedom in dealing with people. He expressed his true feelings to a group of hecklers while he was campaigning with his replacement, Kansas senator Robert J. Dole: the photographers caught him in a classic obscene gesture given with one finger.

Nelson Rockefeller died in 1979 in the company of a twenty-six-year-old female research assistant in his Manhattan townhouse, in circumstances that are somewhat murky and not likely to be cleared up in our time.

Walter Frederick Mondale

Minnesota Liberal

DEMOCRAT
IN OFFICE: 1977–1981
PRESIDENT: JIMMY CARTER

Late in 1974, Walter (Fritz) Mondale dropped out of the race for president saying that he could not face another year of living in the Holiday Inn. That's understandable, but Mondale was also very much aware of his not making much of an impression in the national consciousness—often running behind the "I don't knows" in the opinion polls. Obtaining finances for his campaign was also particularly galling for him; he later opined, "There is no question but that a candidate must necessarily spend more time pursuing dollars for his campaign than he does pursuing policies for his Presidency." What it came down to was that Mondale did not have the kind of overpowering desire to be president that is necessary for a difficult campaign.

Whatever the reasons, Mondale's failure to stay the course meant that his name was very far down on the list of vice-presidential possibilities of the eventual Democratic nominee, Georgia governor Jimmy Carter. Knowing this, Mondale assured Carter when they met that he would campaign hard for the number-two position and that Holiday Inn motel rooms were not so bad now that "they've all been redecorated."

Jimmy Carter had more time than most men in his position to think about his vice-president, since he knew weeks ahead of time that he would be the Democratic nominee. He sent out questionnaires to the various possible candidates asking about "any skeletons in the closet" and requesting complete financial statements. He was looking for someone qualified to be president (naturally), someone with similar views on government, and someone to be a "balance" regionally or ideologically. The field was finally narrowed down to three: Maine senator Edmund Muskie, Ohio senator John Glenn, and Minnesota senator Fritz Mondale. The next step was a personal interview in Plains, Georgia (at the so-called "Court of St. James"). This clinched it for Mondale. When asked later how he had prepared for the interview, he quipped, "The first thing I did was to read the most remarkable book ever written, called *Why Not the Best?* [by Carter]. I found every word absolutely brilliant." So Mondale had a sense of humor. He was also intelligent, a liberal to balance Carter's more conservative views, a government insider who could take some of the sting from Carter's outsider image, and, most important, Mondale was thought qualified to be president.

Carter, it turned out, was so pleased with his selection process that he suggested that in the future, convention delegates should take several days after the presidential

WALTER F. MONDALE
(Collections of the Library of Congress)

nomination to choose a running mate, and then reconvene to vote on the choice.

Mondale was of the predominantly Scandinavian stock of Minnesota and the son of a Methodist minister. While attending Macalester College and just twenty years old, he managed Hubert Humphrey's successful campaign for the Senate from a normally Republican district. Mondale was graduated from the University of Minnesota Law School and in 1960 was appointed to complete the term of the retiring state attorney general. He won another term on his own, and then in 1964 was appointed to fill the U.S. Senate seat of Hubert Humphrey, who was leaving it to become vice-president. He won reelection on his own twice, but there are some Mondale critics who insist that he was appointed to everything, including the vice-presidency.

In the Senate, although there was to be no major legislation bearing his name, his voting record earned him an almost 100-percent rating with the Americans for Democratic Action. Critics said he had supported the war in Vietnam longer than he should have—"the worst mistake of my political career"—and that he was too cautious and pragmatic. When he underwent an appendectomy in 1974, some fellow Democrats were said to be hoping "the surgeon inserted some guts before sewing him up." But his admirers far outnumbered his detractors, and they believed that his reasonableness increased his effectiveness in the Senate.

During the campaign, Mondale took part in the nation's first televised vice-presidential debate, against the Republican nominee, Kansas senator Robert J. Dole. Dole, who had once likened the vice-presidency to "indoor work with no heavy lifting," may have won the contest for sarcastic one-liners, such as his suggestion that George Meany was Senator Mondale's make-up man and that Carter had three positions on everything. But Mondale's measured statements were more appealing in the long run.

Vice-presidents are still completely dependent on the president for their feelings of usefulness, and Mondale was more fortunate than most. He had an office in the White House, an open relationship with Carter's staff, received the same national-security reports as the president, lunched alone with Carter once a week, and spent three to four hours a day with him as part of his open invitation to attend any White House meetings he cared to. He even had some influence in appointments, and pushed his friend Joseph Califano for secretary of Health, Education and Welfare. Some insiders complained that Mondale was too cautious in offering criticism of the president's policies, but this may have been a calculated risk by a man who knew the precariousness of his position.

Mondale was the first vice-president to live in the official vice-presidential residence. In 1974, Congress had finally assigned a home for the second family, in the former home of the Chief of Naval Operations in northwest Washington. He also had a limousine with driver and air force transportation, rated a nineteen-gun salute, and received an annual salary of $65,000 with $10,000 as expense allowance. His net worth before taking office was $77,000, and he joked that he was the only person in government office "who took the job because I needed the money."

George Herbert Walker Bush

"Crisis Manager"

REPUBLICAN
IN OFFICE: 1981–
PRESIDENT: RONALD REAGAN

In 1977, as the Democrats took over in Washington, George Bush ran out of government appointments, and he began to think he might run for president. Two years later, he declared his candidacy and hit the campaign trail. Not too many people knew anything about him, so his set speech consisted largely of an autobiographical outline.

It began with his very Eastern-establishment origins in Connecticut as the son of wealthy onetime (1952–1962) senator Prescott Bush. The family lived in "a barn of a house" in Greenwich and spent summers in Maine. After high school at Andover, George joined the navy, becoming World War II's youngest naval pilot at eighteen. Shot down at twenty, he received the Distinguished Flying Cross and came home a hero. Then it was on to

GEORGE BUSH
(Photographer: Cynthia Johnson. The White House)

Yale, where he earned his degree in economics in two and a half years and membership in Phi Beta Kappa.

Breaking with family tradition, Bush moved to Texas to make his fortune in the oil industry. There he was "bitten by the bug" of politics and served two terms in the House as Houston's first Republican in Washington. When he lost two bids for the Senate, President Nixon appointed him first as ambassador to the United Nations (1970–1973) and then chairman of the Republican National Committee. Under President Ford, he served as United States envoy to Peking and then as director of the C.I.A. Along the way, his name had appeared on a few vice-presidential lists but never made it to the top.

Bush received some very favorable press notices at the beginning of his campaign for the 1977 Republican presidential nomination against Ronald Reagan, but the momentum (Bush called it the "Big Mo") peaked with his win of the Iowa caucus. By any analysis of his record, he was a conservative; but he could never go far enough to the right to suit the hard-liners then dominant in the party. They remained wary of any man in a Brooks Brothers suit. After seeing some of his *un*memorable campaign performances, some people began to think of him as an empty Brooks Brothers suit. His sullen behavior at a New Hampshire debate, too, which in the last moments included all the Republican candidates instead of just Reagan, as Bush had expected, lowered his image even further.

Bush knew the race was hopeless a month before the convention and he dropped out. But he left the door open for the number-two spot. It must have been upsetting for him when, at the last minute, it seemed that former president Gerald Ford would become vice-president again. When Ford had not said no to a polite offer by the Reagan team, events appeared to move rapidly toward what many regarded as the ideal ticket: Reagan–Ford. But there were serious problems. Ford's supporters, who included onetime secretary of state Henry Kissinger, were making demands that would have meant an infringement on the chief executive's powers. Reagan placed a quick call to Bush and then led him before the delegates as his choice for running mate against the incumbents, Carter and Mondale.

As a vice-president vowed to complete loyalty, Bush had to eat a few of his campaign words against Reagan's policies—such as "voodoo economics"—but they were not indigestible. In spite of the great difference in their backgrounds, the two executives have claimed a close personal relationship, and publicly they have had nothing but praise for each other.

Bush has said that if he did not have Reagan's confidence, he would merely be going to funerals in South America. Although he has done everything possible to gain the president's confidence, by becoming the ultimate team player, he has attended several funerals—as well as been present at more positive ceremonial functions. And he was given some definitely major assignments, such as heading up the Presidential Task Force on Regulatory Relief, and was chosen over then–Secretary of State Alexander Haig to be Reagan's "crisis manager."

When a real crisis did occur and Reagan was wounded in an assassination attempt on March 30, 1981, it was Bush who appeared to advantage over Haig's manic declaration "I am in control here." The vice-president conducted business from his own office or his own chair in cabinet meetings, and kept a very low profile—just as all smart and ambitious vice-presidents have done throughout American history.

Diana Dixon Healy, who holds a degree in history, has worked as a writer and researcher. She now lives in Wilton, Connecticut, with her husband, Charles, and their three sons.